CONSCIENCE

OTHER BOOKS BY
DR. O. HALLESBY

———

Prayer

Under His Wings

The Christian Life

Why I Am a Christian

God's Word for Today

CONSCIENCE

BY

O. HALLESBY, Ph. D.

Professor in the Independent Theological Seminary
Oslo, Norway

TRANSLATED BY
CLARENCE J. CARLSEN, M.A.

PUBLISHED BY
AUGSBURG PUBLISHING HOUSE
MINNEAPOLIS, MINNESOTA

CONSCIENCE
Copyright 1933
Augsburg Publishing House

First Edition	December 1933
Second Edition	January 1934
Third Edition	April 1934
Fourth Edition	April 1935
Fifth Edition	January 1936
Sixth Edition	March 1938
Seventh Edition	April 1940
Eighth Edition	September 1941
Ninth Edition	January 1943
Tenth Edition	November 1943
Eleventh Edition	March 1944
Twelfth Edition	November 1944
Thirteenth Edition	January 1945
Fourteenth Edition	February 1946

Printed and Manufactured in the United States of America by
the Augsburg Publishing House, Minneapolis 15, Minnesota
—1795—

Author's Preface

It can scarcely be denied that most of us experience difficulty in getting the *moral* side of our Christian life to keep pace with the *religious* side. The reason for this is not, however, that we emphasize too strongly the religious phase of our relationship to God. We cannot emphasize that too strongly. Our failure lies much rather in not emphasizing the moral aspect enough. As a result our Christian life becomes either dryly *intellectual* or else unduly *emotional,* feverish, and tense. In either event we tend to overlook and to neglect practical, *every-day Christianity.*

It is my desire to deal in this little book with the moral side of the Christian life. I have chosen conscience as my theme because the treatment of this subject affords us a good insight into the nature of the moral life as well as into the practical Christian duties of every-day life.

This book would therefore be a bit of practical theology, a little volume on the cure of souls, a helping hand to folk who experience difficulty with their conscience.

If it will make a small contribution toward the development of a more substantial and conscientious type of Christianity, my desire and my prayer will be fulfilled.

O. HALLESBY.

Publisher's Note

THE Sunday School Times, in a recent issue, said: "The Christian people of America owe a debt of gratitude to the Augsburg Publishing House for bringing to our country and translating this book ('Prayer') by Dr. Hallesby."

The secret of the wonderful appeal which Dr. Hallesby's preaching and writings make to people lies not only in his unusually clear and concise style and presentation but also, and chiefly, in the power emanating from his personal experience and conviction, and in his safe and secure mooring in the Scriptures.

"Conscience" is the fourth in a series of books by Dr. O. Hallesby, professor at the Independent Theological Seminary of Oslo, Norway, that have been brought out in an American edition by Augsburg Publishing House. The first book, "Why I Am a Christian," was published in 1930; the following year we published "Prayer"; in 1932, "Under His Wings," and in 1933, "Conscience."

AUGSBURG PUBLISHING HOUSE.

Contents

What Is Conscience?

"Also he hath set eternity in their heart."
—ECCLESIASTES 3:11.

CONSCIENCE is the simplest and clearest expression of the exalted character and dignity of human life.

Here we touch upon that which makes man a man and exalts him above the animals. In other words, we come in contact with the vital mystery in human life.

This makes it mandatory upon us to remove the shoes from off our feet and tread carefully upon this holy and mysterious ground. This also intimates to us that we shall come upon mysteries which will raise problems that will not only be difficult for us to think our way through, but even more so to express.

But at the same time it also holds out the promise to us that we shall here gain an insight into some of the most marvelous and glorious things in God's whole mighty work of creation. "Also he hath set eternity in their heart," says the ancient sage, as he marvels at the fact that God "hath made everything beautiful in its time."

*

Turning to the sacred Scriptures, the first thing that we notice is that the expression "conscience" is not found in the Old Testament. The thought, however, is there, and is usually expressed by the word "heart." We read in I Samuel 24:5: "And it came to pass afterward, that David's heart smote him, because he had cut off Saul's skirt." This is the case also in II Samuel 24:10, and in several other places. Not until we come to the post-canonical, the so-called apocryphal, books do we find the expression "conscience" used. The Book of Wisdom 17:3 is an illustration.

In the New Testament "conscience" is the expression which is commonly used. And it is used very frequently, especially by Paul and the author of Hebrews. However, we also find the Old Testament expression "heart" used in several instances to denote conscience. Thus in I John 3:19-20: "Hereby shall we know that we are of the truth, and shall assure our heart before him: because if our heart condemn us, God is greater than our heart, and knoweth all things." Here there can be no doubt that heart means conscience. The same is true of Mark 3:5.

The expression "conscience" is derived etymologically from the Latin verb which means to *know with*. It has a corresponding linguistic root in several other languages. Thus in Latin we have *conscientia;* in Greek, *syneidesis;* in Norwegian, *samvite;* and in Swedish, *samvete.* All mean: to know with.

Thus the expression itself, common to many languages, tells us at once that conscience is a knowing with. It is, then, not merely a knowing, a consciousness, but a knowing together with something or some one. Nor need we be in doubt as to what it is that man in his conscience knows together with. Among all races, even the lowest, it is a characteristic of man that he in his conscience knows together with a will that is over and above his own. A supernatural, supramundane, superpowerful will, which makes demands upon the will of man, and which has a right to do so. This will, which is the will of God, is what men call the law or the moral law, that is, the law according to which man's life should be lived. We can, therefore, define conscience as that knowledge or consciousness by which man knows that he is conforming to moral law or the will of God.

Let us note that it is a knowing *with*. It is not merely a knowing of ourselves and a knowing of the will of God. It is a knowing with in the sense that we know that *we* are one *with* the *will of God*. We become conscious of what our relationship is to the will of God, whether we are doing His will or are not doing it. Our conscience tells us, therefore, not only what we *are* but also what we *ought to be*.

In order to understand better what the conscience is, let us compare it with the instinct of animals.

It, too, is a remarkable thing. Instinct tells the animal, in a way that we cannot explain, what to do in order to preserve its own life as well as that of its species. And in a way that is equally inexplicable the animal is warned through its instinct of those things which are dangerous or inimical to its well-being. The instinct of domestic animals has been weakened through association with human beings. In wild animals the instinctive faculty functions with perfect normalcy. We must frequently marvel at their ability to sense danger, such as poison, for instance. As far as we know, wild animals never eat *natural* poisons. We must make use of *artificially* concocted poisons if we would inveigle them into taking it.

But regardless of how precisely and effectively animal instinct functions, it is, nevertheless, nothing more than a *natural* act, as everything else in animal psychology. It functions entirely automatically and by natural necessity.

Conscience, on the other hand, is a knowledge, a consciousness, not, like instinct, an inner compelling urge such as drives the animals and compels them to pursue the course marked out by instinct. Conscience is consciousness of a holy, superhuman law, which addresses itself to man's conscious will, not to enforce obedience to it, but that man might freely and without compulsion follow that law which he through conscience recognizes as the law which he ought to follow.

As a matter of fact, it is through conscience that man acquires consciousness of his humanity, differentiating him from the brute. It is through conscience that man learns that he is not under necessity, as animals are, to follow the natural law, but is ordained to live according to *spiritual* law.

This faculty of knowing with, which man possesses, is exceedingly remarkable.

A sort of doubling of our personality takes place. The I takes a position, so to speak, outside itself and observes itself. Let us note well, too, that it looks at itself in the light of God's will. It looks to see what its own attitude is toward the will of God. And then it pronounces judgment upon itself, upon its own attitude toward the will of God.

Then comes that which is most remarkable of all. The judgment which the I pronounces upon the I is entirely objective and *unbiased*.

A remarkable judgment seat indeed!

In other courts of justice we require that the judge be a disinterested party in the case, fearing that his judgments otherwise might be prejudiced. But at the judgment bar of conscience it is the accused person himself who passes judgment!

As a rule the judgment which is expressed deals with some particular thing which we have done or are about to do, or something that we are saying, thinking, or feeling.

However, it may also pass judgment upon our whole being. At all times it tells us how our actions, words, thoughts, feelings, or what we ourselves are compare with the will of God.

Conscience expresses itself sometimes before, sometimes during, and sometimes after the act involved.

Before it either encourages us to carry out our contemplated action, or advises us not to do so.

During the act the voice of conscience is weakest, as a rule. That is when it is most difficult for conscience to gain a hearing or to make itself heard. We are either preoccupied with what we are doing or are under the sway of passion, with the result that the voice of our conscience is either partly or completely stifled.

After the act conscience usually speaks most strongly, either approving the deed and expressing satisfaction with it, or protesting against it and producing inner unrest and anxiety.

In the former instance we speak of a *good* conscience; in the latter, of a *bad* conscience.

However, these expressions are both misleading, inasmuch as it is not our conscience which is good or bad, but the judgment which it expresses. To be even more exact, it is not the judgment either which is good or bad. My conscience is really equally good whether it expresses approval or disapproval of my act, just as a barometer may be equally good whether it indicates "stormy" or "fair." As a matter of fact, we would have to say that the barometer was a poor one if it always registered "fair." When we speak of a good or a bad conscience, therefore, we mean the effect which its judgment registers upon us, the feeling of pleasure or non-pleasure which it gives us.

How Conscience Functions

"Their conscience bearing witness therewith, and their thoughts one with another accusing or else excusing them."—ROMANS 2:15.

LET us now consider a little more in detail the feeling of pleasure or non-pleasure with which our conscience puts us face to face, the joy and the pain which the functioning of conscience entails. This is very interesting, and throws not a little light upon the peculiar nature of conscience.

We human beings experience joy and pain of widely varying kinds. There are, as it were, various planes of joy and pain, of good and evil, within our physio-psychological being.

First we would mention the lowest plane of good and evil, that, namely, which we associate in particular with our *bodily* existence. We cannot but feel it as a pain, an evil, to be hungry or thirsty. And, conversely, we feel that it is a joyous satisfaction, a good thing, to get food when we are hungry, drink when we are thirsty, and rest when we are weary.

These values we usually group under the general classification: *the pleasant.*

Next we would mention the various kinds of good and evil which we find on the *psychological* plane.

They are of a somewhat higher order. Here it is not a question of gratifying a momentary physical desire. Here it is a psychological need, whether it be a desire for knowledge, honor, influence, power, or wealth that is involved. How many a youth is not possessed with a thirst for knowledge which causes him constant mental distress. And what a delightful satisfaction it is to such a youth when an opportunity at last presents itself to him to acquire knowledge and develop his mental faculties.

These types of good and evil lie on a somewhat higher plane than those we have already mentioned, the sensory. This we see most clearly from the fact that people are willing to deny themselves many bodily pleasures for the sake of gaining mental values such as these. Thus we see many young people sacrifice not only pleasures but even their daily noonday meal in order to be able to acquire an education. And what exertions must not an athlete put forth, what abstinence must he not practice, in order to acquire the proficiency to which he aspires.

All of these many and various kinds of psychological values we usually group together under the one general caption: *the useful*.

Both these types of values, the pleasant and the useful, have this in common that they are valuable in themselves and are sought after only because of the satisfaction they afford.

The physical values satisfy an immediate need. And usually because of this they quickly cease to be a value to us. The cooling breeze is pleasant only as long as I feel warm. Afterwards it quickly becomes unpleasant. The psychological values are by their nature less relative and variable. The satisfaction they afford us is of a more permanent nature. But we seek these values too because of the *advantages* they afford us and the *usefulness* to which we can put them.

Finally, we have an entirely different plane of values, those, namely, which we call *moral* values.

These too satisfy human needs, and must therefore be

termed values. But they are different from all other values, *fundamentally different,* in fact.

Here it is no longer a question of what is pleasant or useful to me, but of what is *right.* Here it is not a question of what I *desire* or *wish,* but of what I *should* or *ought* to do.

Here we recognize, in other words, a value which is *universal* in its nature.

To do right is not a value because it produces a momentary feeling of pleasure, nor because it gives us an advantage for the future. By no means, it is a value in and by itself, not merely in relation to me and my changing needs, be they physical or psychological.

This value is *universal* in its validity. It retains its validity in all the various circumstances of life, whether I am old or young, whether I am hungry or satisfied, whether I am tired or rested. And it is exactly the same with everybody else. And at all times and seasons.

Furthermore, moral values are *absolute* in their nature.

We need only experience a value of this kind and at once all other values become secondary.

It cannot be put on the same level as other values. In the first place, to do right is more important than to satisfy our bodily needs. Moreover, we feel that we must do the right even at the expense of our highest psychological needs. A conscientious person will rather go hungry, freeze, lose his reputation, even his very life, than not to do that which is right.

*

Conscience cannot be deduced from nor explained by other things. It is, in other words, a direct manifestation of that life which makes man a man.

There is, of course, an evolutionistic conception of morality, according to which conscience itself as well as its origin can be accounted for by wholly natural causes, namely, by man's inherent instinct of self-preservation, more specifically, by the "struggle for existence."

According to this view the individual was compelled because of this struggle to band himself together with other individuals and that thereupon, as a result of this so-called process of "natural selection," those elements in society which contained the most individuals capable of sacrificing personal advantage for the sake of the welfare of the group at large emerged from the struggle victorious and survived the others.

According to this view it was the instinct of self-preservation in the individual and in the group which little by little produced those virtues which from time to time were necessary for the preservation of the life of the race.

To begin with these virtues were largely *military,* such as bravery and proficiency at bartering. But gradually society learned from experience that the victorious side also loses in war. Whereupon peaceable intercourse between nations began, and *peacetime* virtues were developed.

Consequently the instinct of self-preservation is the source also of these. The individual as well as society sees that life can be furthered best and made most secure for all when men look upon and treat their fellow men as friends and not as enemies. And those classes of society which do not contain a sufficiently large number of individuals who are capable of doing this will in the long run be submerged in the struggle for existence, according to the law of "natural selection."

Thus men have thought that they could explain

conscience, not only its peculiar nature but its psychological method of operation as well: The experiences of our ancestors have down through the ages deposited themselves in the psyche of the race and have thus entered into and become a part of our instinctive being, all in accordance with the established laws of psychology.

This is then offered as the reason why conscience expresses itself in the *form* that it does. Its remarkable *authoritativeness* and its instinctive *certainty* are both accounted for by its origin, as we have just sketched it.

As animals are warned by inherent instinct not to eat dangerous foods, so man is warned by his inherited instinct, his conscience, not to commit acts which conflict with the fundamental law of his being, the instinct of self-preservation. And each individual and each generation has a part in augmenting this inherited capital, this inherited instinct, and does so every time it suppresses its egoism in favor of the good of the whole.

We feel compelled to state, however, that these ideas are only theories—theories, moreover, that are far removed from the realities of life and directly contradicted by the facts in connection therewith.

The moral history of mankind shows that every great moral epoch has been brought about by individuals who championed causes in opposition to the whole age in which they lived, in fact to the whole past, and who risked their lives in obedience to the truth as they saw it. In this their conviction as to what they deemed to be right they arrayed themselves against the unanimity and wisdom of the cumulative instinct of the race, which opposed them with all the authority of antiquity. Perhaps their contemporaries opposed them besides with outward pressure and coercion.

If we would ask these moral heroes themselves, they would answer with one accord that they acted as they did, not as a result of wise calculations as to what was most advantageous to themselves or others, but, on the contrary, notwithstanding such calculations.

Relative considerations, on the whole, were not what prompted them. They were face to face with the *absolute,* the *eternal.* It was this that *constrained* them to oppose tradition and their own environment. It was this, too, that gave them the *courage* and *power* so to do.

Conscience cannot by any means be explained or accounted for by something else. We cannot say anything more about it than that it is there. And that it is there as a direct manifestation of *personality,* of the *life* of the *spirit.* It is the simple, elementary witness to *eternal* life, for which man was created.

This means that morality is part and parcel of human life in the same way as the *logical* and *esthetical* faculties are. Man's intellect and esthetic sense cannot be accounted for by other things. They can only be pointed out as psychological facts.

So also the moral faculty. In the midst of a world in which everything is relative, limited, and finite, and in which man, too, is reminded, wherever he turns, of his limitations and his finiteness, he is still in touch with a world of an entirely different kind, the realm of the *absolute.*

In his conscience man is confronted by a superhuman, a divine will. Moreover, our experiences with this will are such that we feel absolutely and unconditionally bound to submit to it.

If conscience cannot be accounted for or explained by other things within the realm of human psychology, it follows also that its inner validity cannot be *demonstrated*.

It possesses this characteristic in common with the logical and the esthetical faculties. It is impossible to prove that logical things are logical or that beautiful things are beautiful to those who do not possess the logical faculty or the esthetic sense. Moreover, he who has the logical faculty or the esthetic sense needs no proof. He needs but *experience* the beautiful and he has "proof" enough.

*

We spoke above about a good and a bad conscience. Let us look at this a little more as we proceed to investigate the rôle which *feeling* plays in connection with conscience.

Let us begin by indicating the well-known fact that all the values we have noted above in some way affect our feelings.

Both positively and negatively: I feel *pleasure* when I derive a value, and *non-pleasure* or pain if I fail to derive it.

This is also the case with moral values. And this is just what we mean when we speak of a good and a bad conscience. I experience a feeling of pleasure when I obey the voice of conscience and do what is right. And, conversely, I experience a feeling of non-pleasure or pain when I fail to obey my conscience.

However, there is a distinct difference between the feelings aroused by conscience and those aroused by other values.

This difference comes to light most strongly and clearly on the negative side, that is, in connection with the feeling of *pain*.

If I burn my hand, I feel intense pain. If anybody by slander besmirches my name and honor, the pain is even more intense. But if I inflict an injury upon my moral being, if I knowingly and willingly do wrong, then I feel a pain of an entirely different nature.

It is no doubt impossible to describe exactly the difference between these two kinds of pain, because the feeling of pain connected with morality involves something that is *inexpressible*.

The reason for this is that in our conscience we come face to face with the *absolute*. And this always involves the inexpressible.

In general, we may say that we can apprehend with our thinking and put into words only the lower strata of our psychological experiences. The higher regions are of such an exalted and delicate nature that we cannot think through them clearly, nor can we give expression to them without involving ourselves in contradictions. However, this does not prevent us from experiencing these inexpressible phases of life.

So also with conscience.

There is something inexpressible about the pain associated with an evil conscience. But it can nevertheless be experienced by everybody, even by the least talented. Even primitive man, who has never even heard of such involved concepts as the absolute and the relative, can *experience* the absolute pain of an evil conscience, and know how essentially different it is from all other pain.

Something, however, can be said even about the inexpressible, even though we cannot say everything, perhaps not even the essential things.

In trying to say something about the feeling of pain connected with conscience, we might perhaps express it in

the following way: If I lose a finger, my loss is no doubt
painful enough. But still a relative or limited loss. If
I lose my honor and reputation, I sustain an even more
painful loss. But still this, too, is a limited loss. That
men refuse to accord me their honor and respect does not,
after all, mean such a great deal as long as I do not lose
my own self-respect.

But if I knowingly and willingly act contrary to my
own conscience, then I feel a pain which is *absolute,* and
sustain a loss that is absolute. Then I am no longer losing
something *relative.* Then I lose *all.* Jesus has given
classical expression to this feeling in the words, "For
what doth it profit a man, to gain the whole world, and
forfeit his life?" (Mark 8:36.)

The characteristic thing about the feeling of pain in
connection with conscience is this sense of self-debasement
which we experience when we act contrary to its behests.

Let us note, furthermore, that we do not experience
this sense of self-debasement so much because we *do* the
wrong as because we *will* to do it. That is why an evil
conscience makes one despise, even loathe, oneself. And
this loathing of oneself does not cease at the thought
that one may have the respect of one's fellow men notwithstanding one's inner wretchedness. On the contrary,
this only aggravates it.

As we shall observe later, it is possible for man to
silence his conscience. Consequently it is also possible to
avoid the pain connected with an evil conscience. At least
it is possible to keep it out of our *consciousness.*

But it seems to be impossible for any one to keep it
out of his *subconsciousness.* Recent psychological re-
search into the realm of the subconscious seems to establish this with a certainty which is little short of terrific.

Where conscience is permitted to speak, the pain of

an evil conscience will be experienced in all its gradations, from almost imperceptible restlessness to peacelessness, fear, anxiety, horror, and wildest despair. Suicides bear witness to the fact that the pangs of conscience can become greater than even the dread of death itself. It is these terrible and unendurable pangs of conscience also which compel the criminal to make confession of crimes which the police have not been able to clear up. He prefers any kind of punishment to the torments of his conscience, which he feels that he can no longer endure.

Thus men experience the evil conscience as a foretaste of the everlasting torments of hell.

But the *good* conscience, too, has its peculiar qualities.

The feeling of pleasure which we experience when we heed the voice of conscience surpasses all other feelings of pleasure, if not in intensity at least in quality.

There is something inexpressible about it too. It is impossible to express in words the peculiar joy which we experience when our conscience approves of our actions. A conscientious person is therefore willing to suffer loss of whatsoever kind it may be, of property, honor, limb, yea, even of life itself, rather than lose his good conscience.

A good conscience imparts a new worthwhileness to a person's whole life, gives it a new wealth and fulness, and a quiet, peaceful joy which transcends all other joys. It spreads eternity's sacred halo over even the little details of our temporal existence. And thus gives us a peculiar joy and zest for living, which should be "proof" enough of the truth and validity of the moral life.

As an evil conscience affects adversely our whole life, both physically and mentally, our conscious as well as our subconscious being, so a good conscience is a source of *strength* both physically and mentally. In fact, in many instances it has an outright *healing* effect, not only mentally but physically as well.

And here let us note that a good conscience is not the privilege of the regenerate person only. By no means, the natural man can also experience the joy and blessing which attend a good conscience. If such a person acts in accordance with the dictates of his conscience, he will experience the peaceful joy which the possession of a good conscience affords.

This has been thus ordained by that God "who maketh his sun to rise on the evil and the good, and sendeth rain on the just and the unjust" (Matthew 5:45). God wills to give good gifts to men, because He is love. He gives sinful men, therefore, all the good things that they are willing to accept. And He gives them as many of these good things as He possibly can without their becoming a hindrance to their salvation.

God has therefore willed that unsaved men should enjoy not only the benefits of sunshine and rain, but also the joy of a good conscience.

That such men interpret the good conscience in a wrong way and think that by its aid they can obtain the favor of God and at last eternal salvation, is another side of the matter, one of which we shall speak more presently

The Judgment of Conscience

"For I had not known coveting, except the law had said, Thou shalt not covet."—ROMANS 7:7.

WE speak of the judgment of our conscience. And the expression is an excellent one. For our conscience can really be compared to a *judgment seat.*

Now we know that a judgment seat never has *legislative* authority in any well organized group of human society. It has *judicial* authority only, that is, it can only state whether the action of the accused is punishable according to the law of the land or not. Its duty is to examine the deed in relation to what the law affirms with reference to it, and then decide whether the deed conforms with or violates the law.

This is also what conscience does.

It compares our deeds or our words or our thoughts or our whole being with the moral law, with the will of God. And then pronounces judgment, that is, decides whether we are in conformity or in conflict with the will of God.

This passing of judgment by conscience is so characteristic of it that we shall proceed to look into it a little more closely.

It is in the first place *categorical,* that is, conscience simply expresses its judgment, without giving reasons. This judgment is not based upon previous considerations nor upon wise calculations as to the future consequences of the act. All conscience does is to state simply and clearly whether the act is good or bad.

It is also *absolute.*

Bargaining or compromising is out of the question. It makes no deductions or allowances. If the judgment of my conscience says that the act is good, then the deed must be done. If conscience says that the act is not good, then it must not be done.

Furthermore, it is *individual*.

Let us note in this connection that conscience *functions* in a way that is common to all men, but that the *judgments* of conscience are individual. They concern the individual only, and no one else. I should not, therefore, seek to compel others to accept the judgments of my conscience.

I am not prevented by this, of course, from seeking to *influence* others, whose conscience in my opinion may be in error. It simply means that I should only seek to influence their conscience, until it freely and of its own accord gives them the right guidance. But more of this later.

And, finally, the judgments of conscience are *not appealable*.

When conscience has spoken, its judgment in *that* particular case is irrevocable. Hereby it is not said that conscience cannot experience a development as a result of which its judgment *later* may be different from what it was before. But we shall inquire into that presently in the pages which follow.

Here we wish to underscore the fact that the judgment which my conscience decrees respecting the particular situation in which I for the time being find myself is not appealable. When conscience has spoken, its verdict cannot be altered. It is the *supreme court*. And there is no other court that can quash or annul the judgments of my conscience.

I can, of course, try to evade the inexorable judgment of my own conscience by seeking covert behind the opinions of other people and the judgments of their consciences, judgments which might appear to me to be easier and less severe. But that would not change the categorical and absolute nature of the judgment of my own conscience.

Conscience is no respecter of persons. It gives utterance to its unimpeachable and irrevocable judgments regardless of the outward authority by which it may be confronted. As a matter of fact, it lays down its requirements even to governments and constituted authority: "We must obey God rather than men," Peter said to the authorities of his day when they sought to forbid the apostles to preach the Gospel (Acts 5:29; 4:19).

The *Catholic* Church has an entirely different view of conscience.

From earliest times this Church has had a tendency to enfeeble and weaken the conscience of the individual as well as his individual conviction. This tendency is closely allied with the Catholic conception of the Church and the relation of the individual to that Church.

According to the Catholic conception the Church has been instituted as the intermediary between God and the individual. In this connection we are not thinking of the Church as that spiritual, invisible communion which there is between all those who are born of God and are members of the body of Christ. Not at all. What we mean first and foremost in this connection is the outward church body, namely, the Roman Catholic Church.

The Catholics maintain that their communion and no other is the Church of Christ, because their communion alone possesses the men who can rightly administer the means of grace, the Word and the Sacraments, that is, the only men who may properly mediate the grace and salvation of God to the individual sinner.

These men are the *ordained* priests. Their ordination, it is maintained, gives them this exclusive prerogative because through the so-called apostolic succession it goes back in a direct line to the apostles themselves, who in turn received their ordination at the hands of the Lord. And, it is further maintained, without such ordination no one can preach the Word and administer the Sacraments with *divine* effect. It will in that event be purely a *human* act, without saving efficacy to those to whom it is thus ministered.

But the Roman Catholic Church with its ordained clergy does not act as an intermediary between God and the individual only when it is a question of *grace*. The same is true also when it is a question of the *law* or the will of God. The individual must secure his information concerning the will of God through the Church, which means through the father confessor.

We Protestants would naturally ask at this point: But cannot and should not the individual himself seek to learn what the will of God is by reading the Bible?

Does not the apostle write, "I have not written unto you because ye know not the truth," and "Ye have an anointing from the Holy One, and ye know all things"?

No, it is not that way among the Catholics.

In the first place, it is only so and so as far as the freedom of the individual Catholic to read the Bible is concerned. In the second place, the Catholic Church teaches that it is only the Church, that is, the clergy of the Church, who know how to read the Bible aright. The individual must not, if he would be a loyal Catholic, read anything else out of the Bible than that which the Church prescribes for him.

From this follows Catholic doctrine and practice regarding the conscience.

Just as the individual cannot enter into a personal and independent relationship with God, but always with the Church as the intermediary, so he cannot in his own conscience come face to face with the will of God, but must always go by way of the Church. Which means that he must always be told what to do by his father confessor.

If he has sinned, he cannot personally settle the matter with God by a true confession before Him from out of his own conscience. Not at all. Here again he must go by way of his father confessor. And if he conceals or cloaks a single sin from his confessor, he cannot receive forgiveness for any of his sins.

The *Jesuits* have drawn the logical conclusions from this doctrine of the Catholic Church. They maintain that conscience is in reality nothing but a *prejudicial* attitude. The Jesuitic method of training seeks therefore to assist the individual to overcome, preferably to obliterate entirely, this old, ingrown prejudice and surrender himself wholly and completely to his confessor or his ecclesiastical superiors.

By so doing the individual renounces his own conscience, and leaves all moral considerations and decisions to his confessor.

This doctrine of the conscience is known as *probabilism*.

It does not only deny the ability of the individual to know what is morally right; it denies the very possibility of knowing what is right. For after one has denied that conscience is that within man which gives expression to our relation to the will of God, then we no longer have any *inner* authority to which to adhere. As a result we will vacillate between various *outward* authorities and their divergent opinions as to what is the right thing to do from a moral standpoint in each particular instance.

The Catholic Church, too, lands in probabilism, in spite of its doctrine of ecclesiastical and papal infallibility. For even the great, authorized moral teachers of the Church differ among themselves when teaching the ordinary church member what the will of God is.

The consequence of this is that the Church leaves it to the individual to choose which of these authorized moral teachers of the Church he wishes to follow. And as a consequence of this again it follows very naturally that the individual chooses that teacher of the Church who presents the easiest and most advantageous moral precepts for the various circumstances in life.

This is the great moral morass into which probabilism falls: men no longer ask what is right. They do not even ask which of the moral conceptions with which they are acquainted is right. Nay. They merely ascertain what they in a given case would rather do and then find out if that is probable, that is, whether any teacher of the Church has defended it.

*

On this point, too, Luther rose against the un-Biblical spiritual tyranny of the Roman Church.

He pushed aside the suzerainty of the Church, not only in the *religious* but in the *moral* realm as well.

Just as he brought to light again the Biblical truth concerning *faith,* so also concerning *conscience.* Faith is not, as the Roman Church taught, merely to hold the teachings of the Church to be true; it is the individual soul's personal trust in God's revelation in Christ, mediated by the Word of God alone.

Through this personal meeting with the living God the individual receives not only personal assurance of salvation, of sonship with God, but his conscience also is created anew so that by reading the Word of God he can receive personal assurance as to what the will of God is.

Luther had to fight this battle out first in his own personal life. He had to tear himself loose personally from the moral overlordship which the Church exercised over him as well as over the rest of its members. It is very difficult for us who have never experienced such overlordship to understand what violent struggles Luther had to pass through.

Every time that Luther criticized the doctrines of the Roman Church the Church countered with the one great accusation: Your most serious offense is not that you protest against the teachings of the Church. That many have done before you. No, not at all. Your greatest offense is the *conceit* which you manifest when you set up your own conscience against the whole Church. That is your real sin. For the Church is God's representative on earth. To oppose the Church is to oppose God, and to think oneself above even God Himself and His representative.

Luther relates frequently, too, in his open and candid way, how this thought lay upon his heart like a burden that would crush him. He himself often thought that the whole thing looked unreasonable, that he, a lone man, an insignificant monk, should be in the right, and the old, venerable Church with all its illustrious names should be in the wrong.

He relates also how he again and again was about to agree to a compromise and submit to the authority of the Church over his conscience.

But at the same time he also says that it was God's wonderful leading and inner guidance alone which raised him up again and gave him courage and strength to stand with God, relying upon the testimony of his own conscience alone, with the whole Church against him.

At the Reichstag at Worms, Luther took the final and decisive step in this regard when, speaking before the ecclesiastical and secular authorities assembled there, he said, "My conscience is bound in the Word of God. I cannot and will not recant anything, since it is unsafe and dangerous to act against conscience. Here I stand. I cannot do otherwise. God help me! Amen."

Luther had restored conscience to its Biblical place:

The individual must stand or fall with the convictions of his own conscience. But, be it noted well, not with his conscience alone, but with his conscience *bound in the Word of God*.

By so doing Luther had also restored the Word of God to its proper place:

The individual must live and teach according to the Word of God. But, be it noted well again, according to the Word of God as he himself has become convinced of its truth through his own conscience, enlightened by that Word, not permitting himself to be bound in his conscience by the opinions of others or by their interpretation of the Word of God.

The Conscience of Fallen Man

"By the manifestation of the truth commending ourselves to every man's conscience in the sight of God."—II CORINTHIANS 4:2.

THIS passage of Scripture tells us that every man has a conscience.

The fall into sin has not, then, deprived man of his conscience. In this connection it seems most natural for us to think that conscience is a part of that divine image which, according to the Scriptures, can be found also in fallen man. See II Corinthians 11:7 and James 3:9.

In Paul's writings we find direct statements concerning the conscience of the natural or the unregenerate man: "For when Gentiles that have not the law do by nature the things of the law, these, not having the law, are the law unto themselves; in that they show the work of the law written in their hearts, their conscience bearing witness therewith, and their thoughts one with another accusing or else excusing them" (Romans 2:14-15).

In Romans 1:18ff. the apostle has expressed himself concerning the religious and moral transgressions of the heathen and the wrath of God which because of these is revealed against them. In Romans, chapter 2, where he speaks to the Jews. he calls attention to the fact that there are conscientious heathen, who not only have a certain knowledge of the law, but who in their conscience bind themselves to the law and obey its commandments.

We have a wealth of experience with which to corroborate these words of the apostle.

Our missionaries tell us that in the midst of the religious and moral darkness of heathenism there are individual heathen who have a very sensitive conscience and who live a very good moral life.

Let us note, however, that the apostle, in the passage we have just cited, puts the conscience of the heathen in a class by itself, beside the conscience of the Israelite.

This makes it plain to us at once that the difference between the two is due to the revelation of God, which Israel had received, but the heathen had not. This thought is directly substantiated by the fact that the apostle speaks of the relationship of the conscience to the law. The conscience of the heathen has no other law to adhere to than the one which he feels in his own "heart"; we would say: in his own inherent moral consciousness.

Israel's conscience, on the other hand, had the *revealed* will of God to which to adhere.

There is, therefore, a great difference between the Jew and the heathen, as the apostle points out in Romans 2:12, although both are absolutely alike in *this* respect that they are all sinners and have come short of the glory of God (Romans 3:22-23).

By this the apostle would say that the conscience of man has been damaged by the fall, even though it is present and continues to function even after the fall.

Let us now endeavor to ascertain what it is that remains undamaged in the life of conscience and what it is that has been destroyed by the fall.

The words of the apostle suggest definitely that it is in relation to the law that conscience has been damaged by the fall. As we have previously said, conscience is a judgment seat, and it pronounces its judgments on the basis of definite legal premises which it has at hand. It is this knowledge of the law which the fall has obscured. The apostle has indicated in Romans 1:18-32 how the heathen lost the true knowledge both of God and of the will of God.

It is granted that they have a consciousness of the divine as well as a moral consciousness.

But how great a value the apostle places upon these phases of fallen man he expresses clearly and unmistakably when he says that notwithstanding his religion and morality fallen man is "without God" (Ephesians 2:12). And when he says that "the natural man receiveth not the things of the Spirit of God: for they are foolishness unto him; and he cannot know them, because they are spiritually judged" (I Corinthians 2:14).

As a consequence of his deficient knowledge of the will of God the conscience of the natural man functions deficiently and erroneously in various ways. This we have abundant opportunity to observe in the moral and religious life of the heathen, both in the past and in the present.

Thus we observe that religiously the conscience of the heathen leads him in his worship to bow down to manmade things instead of to the Creator and to perform the emptiest and most meaningless kinds of ceremonialism.

We observe also that the conscience of the heathen approves of acts in connection with divine worship which are openly immoral, such as sexual license in the temple in honor of the gods.

We observe furthermore that it forbids acts which are morally permissible, such, for instance, as the eating of horse meat; or it forbids acts which are morally good, as for instance to help the sick who have been made ill by the curse of the deity, as they think.

And, finally, we observe that the conscience of a heathen can require him to do things which are manifestly immoral, such, for instance, as to murder his father's murderer.

Generally speaking, it is no doubt correct to say that it is due to the fall in sin that conscience expresses itself so exceedingly divergently as it does in various individuals and peoples and at various times. The divergent, in fact, oftentimes contradictory, decrees expressed by conscience are a consequence of sin, which has weakened and distorted conscience.

*

Such mutually contradictory judgments of conscience as these have been the source of many intellectual difficulties. Some have seen in them proof that conscience is not of that absolute nature as we have pictured it above. In their opinion these divergencies prove that conscience is nothing but a kind of inherited instinct. The fact that this instinct expresses itself so divergently, in fact so contradictorily, can be accounted for, they maintain, by the divergent outward and inner circumstances under which the different peoples and races have lived during the thousands of years during which this instinct was being developed.

I have shown above that this conception of conscience as an inherited natural instinct is entirely incompatible with the psychological nature and history of conscience. See page 20 above.

But even though it is clear to us that these differences cannot be accounted for in this way, the problem itself is as far from being solved as it ever was.

There is still another consideration, which makes the problem even more difficult. Thus we observe that *for-*

mally the conscience always functions in precisely the *same* way, regardless of how *divergent* its judgments may be.

We notice that the conscience of the heathen obligates him to murder his father's murderer. The Christian's conscience says: Thou shalt love thy enemies, be willing to forgive them thyself, and ask God to forgive them. But we notice at the same time that conscience expresses itself just as categorically, just as absolutely, just as inexorably in the heathen as in the Christian.

At first glance this fact has a disturbing effect upon all of us.

But the problem is solved as soon as we give full consideration to the fact that conscience is a *judgment seat* in man.

As a judgment seat does not *make laws* but only *passes judgment,* so also conscience. It pronounces judgment always on the basis of that knowledge of the will of God which the person concerned is in possession of at the time.

And since the heathen, as indicated above, have a very deficient knowledge of the will of God, their conscience will, therefore, of necessity, pronounce an entirely different judgment from that of the conscience of a Christian, which through the supernatural revelation of God has received full knowledge of the will of God.

As soon as this becomes clear to us we see that the somewhat disturbing fact which we have discussed above throws light on a very important aspect of conscience.

It tells us that we not only can but should distinguish between the *form* and the *content* of conscience. By content we mean here the concrete substance of the judgment which conscience pronounces. And by the form of conscience we mean that peculiar function of the soul which tells man that he ought to do the will of God.

Now notice the very important fact, which we have previously indicated, that conscience according to its form is *absolutely the same* in all men, in all peoples, in all ages. It is right to say, therefore, that according to its form conscience is *infallible*.

In all men it speaks with unimpeachable authority and says that we ought to submit to the absolute will of God.

According to its content, on the other hand, conscience is *not* infallible. For the content of the judgment which conscience pronounces is dependent upon the extent of the knowledge of the will of God which the individual possesses.

This gives us greater insight into the consequences of the fall as it affects the conscience.

We see now that God in His mercy has so ordained it that in fallen man, too, there is a voice, a voice which speaks to him with absolute authority from the invisible realm of eternity, and which intuitively tells him that he ought to do the will of God.

This does not mean, of course, that the *form* of conscience has not been damaged at all by the fall. Though it has been damaged less than the content of conscience, nevertheless it has been damaged by the fall. Its voice has lost much of its *strength* as well as its *clarity*.

In what it says, namely, that we ought to do the will of God, it is right and wholly unimpeachable. But the strength with which it says it has, as a rule, been diminished a great deal. And it does not become of such *decisive* importance in the life of the individual as it should be by its nature.

If it is a voice from *eternity* in the midst of our temporal life, then it is clear that it should speak the authoritative word in our lives. We should listen to it at every step we take. Its voice should speak the authoritative and final word in all the various circumstances of life.

Conscience has been called the *voice of God*.

From what we have now observed it is clear that this is an unfortunate expression, if we think of conscience as a whole, namely, of both the form and the content of conscience. For, as we have seen, its judgments are both divergent and contradictory. If it were the voice of God, it could not, of course, contradict itself.

But if we think of the *form* of conscience, that function of soul which intuitively and unmistakably tells us all that we ought to do the will of God, then we can well designate it as the voice of God. God Himself has ordained that these regular admonitions should come to us from the realm of the absolute and the eternal. Admonitions which we experience without ourselves doing anything to bring them about. In fact, most people do not a little to rid themselves of this voice of God within.

Conscience and the Word of God

"Having our hearts sprinkled from an evil conscience."—HEBREWS 10:22.

WE have now seen that it is his imperfect knowledge of the will of God that constitutes the real deficiency in connection with the conscience of the heathen.

This accounts also for the fact that there are large areas in the life of a heathen concerning which his conscience does not express itself at all. Thus we observe that his conscience expresses itself only about the particular things in his life, such as his actions, his words, his thoughts. About his whole being, about the attitude of heart from which his thoughts, words, and deeds proceed, a heathen's conscience seldom if ever expresses itself.

It is true that there are instances in which the conscience of a heathen will express itself about the nature of his whole being, and not only about particular deeds or words. But when it does, it speaks, not of the *moral* nature of his person, but of his *ceremonial* uncleanness.

By ceremonial uncleanness we mean an uncleanness which is due, not to a moral condition, but to purely *natural* conditions or acts, which, according to the laws governing worship, render one unfit to officiate at or participate in worship, until the ceremonial uncleanness has been removed by some act of cleansing or other, as prescribed by the laws involved.

In the Old Testament, too, we find this distinction between moral and ceremonial uncleanness.

Thus we read in Leviticus, chapter 12, that a woman shall be ceremonially unclean for 33 days when she has borne a man-child and 66 days when she has borne a maid-child. "She shall touch no hallowed thing, nor come into the sanctuary, until the days of her purifying be fulfilled." "And when the days of her purifying are fulfilled, . . . she shall bring a lamb a year old for a burnt-offering, and a young pigeon, or a turtle-dove, for a sin-offering, unto the door of the tent of meeting, unto the priest: and he shall offer it before Jehovah, and make atonement for her; and she shall be cleansed. . . ."

The primary deficiency, and the vital one, in the conscience of the heathen is, then, that it cannot distinguish the will of God clearly enough to see that man should be judged according to the *moral foundation* of his whole being, according to the sinful state of soul from which all his particular sins proceed.

We must also make mention of another defect in the conscience of the heathen, namely, that it judges even his particular words and deeds very imperfectly. May I call attention here to the erroneous moral decisions of the heathen which I have referred to above: ceremonial immorality in the temple and blood-revenge, to mention the most notorious ones. Besides these we could of course make mention of a multitude of lesser moral aberrations.

To save the race which had fallen into sin God could not, therefore, make use of conscience alone.

We shall see later that conscience is not able to change the sinful foundation of man's being, that which the Bible calls the *heart*.

Meanwhile we would underscore the fact that the conscience of fallen man alone is not able to convince man of his sinfulness. It is true that he can in his conscience sense the fact that he is committing sin, and that against both God and man. But fallen man cannot learn to know the true nature and eternal import of sin through his conscience alone.

And the reason is, as indicated above, simply this, that fallen man has lost the true knowledge of the will of God.

It was necessary for God, therefore, to *reveal* Himself to fallen man. That is what the Bible tells us from cover to cover.

Moreover, we learn from the Bible that the first thing God had to reveal was the *law*. "For the law was given through Moses; grace and truth came through Jesus Christ" (John 1:17; Luke 16:16).

The one people which God had chosen unto Himself was given the knowledge of the will of God in a way in which none of the heathen nations had received it, both with regard to divine worship: the sacrifices and the atonement, and with regard to the moral life.

But God's revelation had to be given step by step.

He could not give them the full Gospel light all at once. And the revelation of the law had to be given in the same way. God has employed masterly pedagogical wisdom. We teach our children by dividing up the subject-matter of education into a number of grades, running throughout a number of years. If we were to thrust all the subjects upon the child during the very first year, the child would become completely bewildered, and the result would be that he would not learn anything. But if we give the instruction gradually, in such a way that each portion of it is related to and is based upon the preceding, then the child will be able to follow along and will, after he has passed all the grades, have acquired it all.

This was the method that God employed also when He

enrolled Israel, that nation-child, into the school of His revelation, and conducted him through grade by grade.

Now and then the Israelites would be disobedient and rebellious, and would refuse to learn anything in the class to which they had been promoted. Then they would have to be put back and take the grade over again. But God was compassionate and patient with His children, even though they were disobedient and not very willing to learn. And up through the centuries He finally succeeded in teaching His chosen people more and more of His will, until He at last could promote it to the *highest* class, that which began just as the *fulness of time* had come.

*

Up to this time God had spoken by divers portions and in divers manners through the prophets, but now He sent His own Son to complete and bring to a consummation the revelation of God, including the revelation of His law, or will.

For we are told very clearly in the New Testament that the Old Testament revelation of the will of God was both insufficient and imperfect. In this connection see Hebrews 9:9-10: "According to which are offered both gifts and sacrifices that cannot, as touching the *conscience,* make the worshipper perfect, being only (with meats and drinks and divers washings) *carnal ordinances,* imposed until a time of reformation."

Here we are told that the imperfect thing about the Old Covenant revelation of law is the carnal ordinances. And by them are meant the *outward* precepts. Moreover, the author mentions specifically the things he has in mind, namely, the many ordinances concerning meat and drink, the things they had permission to eat and the things they did not have permission to eat.

And lo, we are in the midst of *ceremonial* uncleanness, an uncleanness which has nothing whatsoever to do with morality, only with purely natural things. Now, the trouble with these precepts is that they do not inquire into the *attitude of heart,* the *motive,* of the person. It is the outward act itself which is considered sinful. It is therefore just as sinful and is punished just as severely whether it is done intentionally or by mistake.

As an illustration of this we might mention Uzzah, who helped transport the ark of God when David wanted it brought to Jerusalem. The oxen that were being driven became restive as they came near to the threshing floor of Nacon, and the ark was about to fall out of the cart. Then Uzzah took hold of the ark and steadied it, so that it would not fall. "And the anger of Jehovah was kindled against Uzzah; and God smote him there for his error; and there he died by the ark of God" (II Samuel 6:3-7).

His error was that he touched the ark, which, according to Numbers 4:15, no one was permitted to do except upon pain of death.

Most of us no doubt take offense at this.

We cannot help asking: Why did God deal so harshly with this man, who, after all, was not intent upon doing evil at all, but, on the contrary, was intent upon doing a good deed, namely, preventing the ark of God from being damaged, perhaps even destroyed?

Why was God on the whole concerned about outward precepts of this kind? They did not in any way take motive into account.

And what was the object of such severe punishment as this? To us most of the punishments visited upon the Israelites seem inordinately severe.

Of course, we have no assurance that we shall ever have all our questions answered.

But God is righteous in all that He does, even though we cannot always comprehend Him. To be incomprehensible is a part of His very nature as God. And when a God whose ways are past finding out reveals Himself, there must be something about His revelation which we cannot comprehend.

But a *little* we do seem to comprehend even here.

Any one who has the least knowledge of child training knows that we cannot speak to a *little* child about *motives* and *attitudes*. The little one does not understand such things. What the child can understand is the *act itself* and whether he has done what he was told to do by his father and mother, or has refrained from doing what he was told not to do.

In *early* life a child develops obedience in just that way, by doing what his father and mother tell him to do without knowing the why and the wherefore of it. Without any debate between parent and child as to why the child must do thus and so and not otherwise.

This is exactly the way God dealt also with that nation-child which He had adopted and begun to bring up. The first and foremost thing that He had to teach the children of Israel was unconditional obedience. That is why He gave them very clear and definite commandments and precepts of an *outward* nature—and required that they be *punctiliously* observed.

There is this to be noted about the severe punishments that He ordained, that they constituted an effective *object-lesson,* which impressed upon this nation-child better than words could do that which it above all else had to learn: that God is a holy God and that His will is inviolable. It was therefore a capital offense to disobey the commandments which God had given.

*

We might also mention *polygamy* as an illustration of that which was imperfect in the Old Testament revelation of law. True, polygamy was never at any time either per-mitted or forbidden in the law. But the law did presup-pose it, took it for granted (Deuteronomy 21:15). The only thing that the law forbade was, that the king shall *multiply* wives to himself, that is, have *many* wives (Deuteronomy 17:17).

We might mention further the *bill of divorcement* which Moses upon God's command gave to the people (Deuter-onomy 24:1-4). About this Jesus says in Matthew 19: 1-9 that it was given because of the people's hardness of heart, and that it is really not an expression of the will of God regarding the married estate.

Further, we might mention the so-called *imprecatory psalms,* in which the author desires and prays for revenge and retaliation against his enemies: "Happy shall he be, who rewardeth thee as thou hast served us. Happy shall he be, that taketh and dasheth thy little ones against the rock" (Psalm 137:8-9).

That this attitude toward one's enemies is imperfect is easy to see, especially when we compare it with the attitude of Jesus toward His enemies. He wept over rebel-lious and bloodthirsty Jerusalem. And on the cross He prayed for His executioners: "Father, forgive them; for they know not what they do!" To His disciples He said, "Love your enemies, and pray for them that persecute you" (Matthew 5:44).

There is, then, something imperfect about these psalms of revenge.

We should observe, meanwhile, that when the psalmist gives expression to these terrible desires respecting his enemies, he does not do so from a desire for *personal* revenge. It is upon the enemies of *God's people* that he

desires these terrible visitations. Moreover, the fact that
he desires this must be looked upon as an imperfect expression on his part of faith in God's *righteousness*.

The most distressing thing to the believing Israelite was
not the persecutions which the ungodly instituted against
him. It was rather that God kept silence in the face of
injustice of this kind, so that the ungodly could blaspheme
with great boldness and say, "Where is your God? He
does not visit His wrath upon us no matter how much
evil we do against you."

At such a time the faithful were in danger of losing
their very faith in God. Note, by way of illustration,
Asaph's touching confession in Psalm 73:2-14. That was
when the desire and prayer was born within him that God
would show Himself as God and make good His threats
as well as His promises, His threats against the ungodly
and His promises to the faithful.

But even though we look at these psalms in this light,
we are compelled to say even then that they are, after all,
only an imperfect expression of the will of God. To Jesus
the important thing was the *salvation* of His enemies, not
their *punishment*.

We have now noted the most important deficiencies in
the Old Covenant's knowledge of the will of God. And
we conclude these thoughts by calling attention again to
the passage we cited, Hebrews 9:9-10, that the Old Testament revelation of law could not make the worshipper of
God perfect as touching the *conscience*. It could not, in
other words, make the conscience *perfect* in its relation to
God.

*

That is why God intervened with a New Covenant, the
concluding and final revelation of God. Also the concluding revelation of the law of God, of the will of God.

Jesus was conscious of the fact that He was the One who was to complete the Old Covenant revelation of divine law: "Think not that I came to destroy the law or the prophets: I came not to destroy, but to fulfil" (Matthew 5:17).

This passage must not, meanwhile, be interpreted as though Jesus meant that the Mosaic ordinances were to retain their validity in the New Covenant. By no means. He has clearly stated that the outward, the statutory, aspects of the Mosaic ordinances were to be abrogated, and that both religiously and morally, that is, both when it was a question of man's relation to God as well as his relation to his fellow men.

The abrogation of the Old Testament laws pertaining to *divine worship* was intimated when Jesus said, "Woman, believe me, the hour cometh, when neither in this mountain, nor in Jerusalem, shall ye worship the Father" (John 4:21).

When, therefore, Jesus says that He is not come to destroy the law, He no doubt means that He is not come to set at nought God's previous revelation, but to continue it and complete it. He is come to fulfil and to accomplish all things which were promised in the law and in the prophets, not only by His words, but also by symbolic observances and ordinances. As Philip said to Nathanael, "We have found him, of whom Moses in the law, and the prophets, wrote" (John 1:45).

*

What is now that *new thing* which Jesus brought in connection with the revelation of the will of God?

In the first place, He preached the new and revolutionary truth that sin does not consist fundamentally in the deeds we do, nor in the words we speak, but in the attitude of heart from which these proceed.

He says, for instance, "For from within, out of the heart of men, evil thoughts proceed, fornications, thefts, murders, adulteries, covetings, wickedness, deceit, lasciviousness, an evil eye, railing, pride, foolishness" (Mark 7:21-22).

Here Jesus says that what makes a deed good or bad, sinful or not sinful, is not the *doing* of it, nor its *consequence,* nor its *result,* but the motive, the *impelling purpose* which gives rise to it. Sin is therefore primarily and basically a condition of our heart, an expression of our will.

This Jesus brings out by means of various illustrations in the Sermon on the Mount. See Matthew 5:23-24; 6:1-6.

Even our best deeds, such as to sacrifice, to pray, and to do alms, are worthless from a moral standpoint unless they proceed from a right attitude of heart. If I do alms for the purpose of gaining honor and recognition from men, the one who receives my gift will, of course, be benefited by it; but as far as I myself am concerned the deed will not only be morally worthless, it will be morally evil, because it sprang from the wrong motive.

In the second place, Jesus proclaimed the new truth that our real sins are our inner sins, that we have really committed sin as soon as we have yielded to sin within.

"Ye have heard that it was said to them of old time, Thou shalt not kill; and whosoever shall kill shall be in danger of the judgment: but I say unto you, that every one who is angry with his brother shall be in danger of judgment" (Matthew 5:21-22). "Ye have heard that it was said, Thou shalt not commit adultery: but I say unto you, that every one that looketh on a woman to lust after her hath committed adultery with her already in his heart" (Matthew 5:27-28).

Jesus has herewith brought the revelation of God forward to the place which God had in mind from the very beginning of the Old Covenant. Because of their hardness of heart God had not been able to tell them these things before. That was why He had to give commandments and precepts concerning outward acts, sinful words likewise, and even concerning sinful thoughts.

Jesus was the first to throw the light of the law into the place it was really intended to reach, into the heart of man, his will, his motives. Now the light of God's law is focused, not upon particular phases of human life only, but upon man himself.

And concerning man Jesus says, not only that he *does* evil, and *speaks* evil, and *thinks* evil, but that he *is* evil (Luke 11:13).

And the evil thing about us is that what we do, say, and think always centers about ourselves. It is about ourselves we are always concerned.

Jesus, on the other hand, was free from sin. He was good. In all of life's relationships He did, not His own will, but the Father's. He loved His neighbor as Himself at all times, and never thought of Himself if others needed His help.

Jesus threw new light also upon our relationship to God.

The heathen all speak of *worshipping* God, *serving* God, or *sacrificing* to God. Jesus, however, speaks of *loving* God. "Thou shalt love the Lord thy God with all thy heart, and with all thy soul, and with all thy mind" (Matthew 22:37).

Also in our relationship to God, therefore, it is our *attitude of heart* that counts. No matter how pious the acts may be which we perform, such as prayer and sacrifice, they may be entirely worthless, Jesus says (Matthew 5:23-24; 6:5-6). Jesus looks to the hearts of those who seek Him.

This Paul gives expression to in the following way, "And if I have the gift of prophecy, and know all mysteries and all knowledge; and if I have all faith, so as to remove mountains, but have not *love,* I am nothing" (I Corinthians 13:2-3).

We have now traced the main course of God's revelation of His holy law.

As we all know, God's revelation of *law* is a part of His revelation of *salvation.* It is the primary, the foundation part, of God's salvation. For salvation is salvation from sin. The worst aspect of man's sin is not that he has committed sin, but that he does not realize and acknowledge his sinfulness.

Through the revelation of His law, God has now provided the conscience of fallen man with that law-material which must come first and which is absolutely indispensable if conscience is to be able to convict men of sin.

Now it is only a question of conscience *using* this law-material.

Had the conscience not been damaged, it would have begun to make use of this law-material at once, as soon as it had acquired knowledge of it. But here we see in all its fulness how the conscience of fallen man has been *damaged.*

In Christian countries all normal people have, of course, acquired a knowledge of the law revealed through Jesus Christ, that is, of the will of God. We note, however, that most of them live as though they had never had any such knowledge whatsoever. Their conscience is unable to make their daily lives conform to the divine light.

Now, this could be interpreted to mean that they all had *heard* the clear voice of conscience and had felt that their life stood condemned in the light of Biblical truth, but that they had *refused* to submit to the dictates of their conscience.

However, the thing cannot be explained in quite that way. For if that were the case these people would be going about their daily tasks with the judgment of a pierced conscience hanging over them. The very fact that they have refused to humble themselves would cause them to feel the pain of the inexorable judgments and the crushing accusations of their conscience.

But that is just what most of them do *not* feel.

The most terrifying fact with which we are daily confronted in Christian lands is that most people live at odds with their conscience, and in comparative unconcern. It does not appear that they feel any crushing judgment of conscience upon themselves.

We shall now proceed to inquire into that which the salvation of God must do in this connection.

The Awakening of Conscience

"How much more shall the blood of Christ, who through the eternal Spirit offered himself without blemish unto God, cleanse your conscience from dead works to serve the living God."—HEBREWS 9:14.

WE have now seen that the conscience of fallen man is not helped by the fact alone that God through Christ has revealed His will to man. Before the conscience of man can derive any benefit from the revelation of the divine will, God must perform a *miracle* with our conscience.

This miracle we call *the awakening.*

Spiritual awakening is nothing else but the awakening of the *conscience.* God touches our conscience by one means or another in such a way that it begins to function normally. Up to this time it has been more or less dormant. At times it has even failed to give expression to its judgments. At other times it has spoken so feebly and indistinctly that it has been neither heard nor heeded.

Then something happens.

What it is that happens and how it happens, is not so easy to say.

Spiritual awakening is on the whole one of the most mysterious things in life.

But the *workings* of this mysterious act which God performs within us are not so difficult to observe.

These workings may be very gradual, they may also be very rapid, even sudden; but the effect of the miracle by which God brings about our awakening is nevertheless the same: we feel that we have been made to *stand before God* in a wonderful way.

The relation between this experience and our conscience is indeed remarkable.

Our conscience speaks to us without our asking it to do so or desiring it. As a matter of fact, it speaks to us even when we would prefer to have it remain silent. And perhaps never more authoritatively than just at such a time.

Precisely the same is the case with our spiritual awakening. It comes without our asking it, or desiring it. Indeed, when it does come, we feel very uncomfortable about it, every one of us, because we feel that it comes so inopportunely.

Here we note the gracious aspect of spiritual awakening, the *unmerited* phase of it.

We are not awakened because we have desired it or willed it or prepared ourselves for it. On the contrary, we do one thing prior to our awakening, and this one thing is to try to *hinder* it, or, to be more exact, to make it as difficult as possible for God to awaken us.

But God is able, nevertheless, to perform the miracle of spiritual awakening within us. He intervenes, without asking our permission to do so.

Obviously, this does not mean that God *compels* any one to become a Christian. We are speaking here of awakening, not repentance. God does not compel any one to repent. But He has reserved the right to awaken us, and that without asking our permission. He permits none of us to take the broad road to eternal perdition without being called to a halt enroute by the living God, who through the miracle of spiritual awakening gives us the possibility of becoming repentant.

There are some remarkable passages in the Scriptures about God *giving* repentance to man. See, for instance, Acts 5:31; 11:18; II Timothy 2:25. In fact, we are even told here that He gives repentance even as He gives the remission of sins.

Let us note, moreover, that it is through spiritual awakening that God gives man repentance. Through the miracle of awakening God works upon our wills until we ourselves will to become repentant.

In the Scriptures we find this thought expressed thus: "It is God who worketh in you both to will and to work for his good pleasure" (Philippians 2:13). "And a certain woman named Lydia . . . heard us: whose heart the Lord opened to give heed unto the things which were spoken by Paul" (Acts 16:14).

We have seen that the expression "heart" is used both in the Old and in the New Testament in the sense of "conscience." In this case also it seems to lie near at hand to understand "heart" in that sense. In that event we would read that God opened the conscience of Lydia so that she gave heed to the Word.

Here we see, then, how God proceeds when He works within us to will. He works through our conscience. He "opens" our conscience.

How He opens our conscience, that is the miracle of spiritual awakening, a divine mystery. But *that* He opens it, we can all experience by His grace.

What are the resultant *effects* when God opens our conscience?

The first and most immediate effect is no doubt that conscience begins *to reassert itself*.

Before, it was more or less dormant. Even when it did speak, its voice was very faint. And as a result it was not heeded. Perhaps it was even forcibly hushed into silence.

Now it is permitted to reassert itself. In fact it is permitted to speak the *final* word, which it according to its nature should be permitted to speak.

It is by a miracle of God that our conscience is thus given permission to speak the authoritative word. We feel that we have been transported *into the very presence of the all-seeing God.*

But are we not there all the time?

No, that is just what we are not. We are here dealing with sacred and mysterious things, which are not easy to understand. Scripture speaks about seasons "when he may be found" and "when he is near" (Isaiah 55:6).

Here we have the real mystery in connection with seasons of spiritual awakening, the grace of God connected therewith.

It is in such holy seasons as this and when we are in such a holy place as in the presence of God that our conscience is again restored to its rightful element and is enabled to do what it is supposed to do.

Now it can speak with authority, yea, with power.

Now it is in truth the voice of God! The voice which pierces through our very bone and marrow.

The Scriptures speak of people who tremble at the word of the Lord (Isaiah 66:2). This is just what the awakened soul now experiences. Now he understands the words of the psalmist: "Thou, even thou, art to be feared: And who may stand in thy sight when once thou art angry" (Psalm 76:7).

The awakened soul not only hears the voice of God; he also feels that the eye of God is upon him. So nigh has the Lord drawn unto him. In fact, he often feels as though God sits and looks right down upon his life, both night and day.

*

Permit a little parenthetical remark at this point.

Many an awakened soul in our day will no doubt feel that he is somewhat of a stranger to the things we have here considered. That is because there are so many kinds of awakenings in our day. Oftentimes awakenings are nothing but waves of emotionalism. Or soul-shocks, induced by a strong human will. When such is the case we cannot expect to find any of the effects which a genuinely *Biblical* awakening produces *in the conscience.*

To this we must add that there is very little awakening power even in some spiritual awakenings which are otherwise sound and good.

Looking at these things soberly, we must admit that there was more *power* in the spiritual awakenings of by-gone days. Not that the awakenings were greater in those days. On the contrary, we in our day are more efficient when it comes to promoting spiritual awakenings. But that there was more power inherent in the awakenings of the past is apparent from the fact that they affected the consciences of men more profoundly and brought forth a deeper consciousness of sin.

Meanwhile, permit me to interject another thought so as to obviate misunderstanding.

In every spiritual awakening there are some who attain peace and joy with comparative ease. In their case it all takes place not only within a comparatively brief space of time, but also without very much of a struggle. When these people read what I am here writing about the struggle, anxiety, and distress connected with spiritual awakening, they may become disorientated and confused.

In this connection I would call attention to the fact that the manner in which spiritual awakening takes place in its earlier stages is of lesser significance. Some enter upon a period of *distress* at once. Others go through only a brief struggle to begin with, and then experience a season full of light, exalted emotions, and inner peace. However, as a rule, before long these people, too, must pass through a period of storm and stress. And oftentimes we observe that they experience a harder struggle than those who were thrown immediately into great distress of soul.

Permit me at this point to interject still another remark.

The description I am about to give of the struggles connected with spiritual awakening, repentance, and faith must not be misunderstood. I do not mean to say that an awakened soul can *observe* all these things in himself at the time of his awakening and can consciously *reflect* upon them as I shall describe them.

Not at all, as I shall emphasize again and again, the awakened soul *experiences* much more than he *understands,* much more than he by self-observation is able to comprehend. But he *experiences* it to the full nevertheless. *Afterwards* he can by self-observation clarify the whole process in his own thinking. And that is what I would like to help him do.

It is, of course, a well known phenomenon in life in general that we experience more than we at the moment can apprehend clearly with our minds.

What is it, then, about which conscience speaks to the awakened soul?

About two things only, about the will of God, and about the sin which the awakened soul has committed.

Which particular sins it speaks about depends upon how

much the awakened soul knows about the will of God. As a rule this is not such a great deal in the early stages of his awakening.

Conscience will, therefore, to begin with, judge with respect to his outward sins, such as lying, cheating, cursing, drinking, dancing, manifestations of violent temper, sulkiness, contrariness, and so on.

But the awakened soul will soon acquire more knowledge of the will of God. He will naturally begin to pray, to read the Bible, to hear the Word of God, and to seek advice from other believers. And it will not be long before his conscience will begin to judge him also with respect to his *inner* sins, his sins of thought, desire, and imagination.

The sway of his conscience has thus been extended tremendously, and it now judges him unceasingly, all day long.

After some time the awakened soul's knowledge of the will of God is further increased and his conscience begins to judge him with respect to another phase of his life, his *sins of omission,* the things which he could and should do each day toward others, but which he neglects to do.

Finally, the awakened soul will, through the Word of God, become so enlightened that his conscience will not only judge him with respect to his particular sins, in thought, word, deed, desire, and imagination as well as of omission, but *his whole person,* his heart, from which all particular sins spring forth, as fresh shoots from a strong root.

And as soon as conscience has begun to reach into the heart with its judgments, then it has begun in all earnestness to judge him in part and in whole. For now he knows that God does not look only to the right act

and the right word. It is the *motive* back of what he says
and does which really counts before God.

And now his conscience tells him with inflexible honesty and inexorable authority: you do not love God!
Neither do you love your fellow men. You love only yourself and those people that you can make use of to your
own profit or enjoyment.

Your conscience continues to speak plainly: you pray
to God, true enough, but do you love God, you who must
force yourself to speak with God even for a few moments,
and who feel happy and relieved when you have dis-
charged what is to you an arduous duty?

In fact, you do not even think about God during the
brief space of time that you are speaking with Him. Your
thoughts go off in all directions, so much so that it requires a great exertion of will on your part to pray the
Lord's Prayer through to the end without allowing your
thoughts to stray away from God.

You read the Word of God also.

But do you love God, you who must force yourself to
read even a single chapter of the Bible each day, and
besides find that it is difficult enough even then to con-
centrate upon what you are reading? The newspaper on
the other hand—how willingly and with what great inter-
est you read it! In fact, you cannot dispense with it without feeling that you are missing a great deal.

You struggle against your sins, too.

But do you *hate* sin? No; you love it. It is only because you are afraid of its consequences that you refrain
from it. You are afraid that your conscience will torment
you. And you are especially afraid of the eternal torments.

You are sorry for your sins, too.

But are you *penitent?* Nay; the sorrow which you feel

because of sin is nothing but that which the Scriptures speak of as "the sorrow of the world," which is the egoist's sorrow because of the fact that sin has dangerous and destructive consequences.

*

Let us pause here for a moment and look at the miracle which God has performed in the conscience of this awakened soul.

Through the Word of God this awakened person has not only learned to *know* the will of God, the whole will of God, which says simply and plainly, thou shalt love the Lord thy God with all thy heart, and thy neighbor as thyself.

He has also begun to *feel* it.

His newly awakened conscience has brought the law to bear upon his inmost being, not merely as theoretical knowledge but as the most actual reality, as the divine will which claims absolute sovereignty over man and which *should* therefore be complied with forthwith.

Hereby the awakening has reached its goal.

Through this awakening God has now made possible the *conversion* of the awakened soul. The latter must now choose. He is free to choose *whatever* he wills. But he *must* choose. And there is only one of two things to choose. *Either* to take offense at God and the truth which He has revealed to him through his conscience. In which event he proceeds at once to silence his conscience. Some employ force in seeking to accomplish this, others deception. But more about this later.

Or the awakened soul submits to the truth of which he has become inwardly convinced through the Word of God and his new-born conscience.

In which event a remarkable thing takes place.

At the very moment that the awakened soul makes this decision to repent he performs the first act of *faith.*

He believes in the law of God.

Let us now observe what a heroic faith this is.

He not only believes that what the Scriptures say concerning the will of God is true. Nor does he believe only in a hazy way, so to speak, that this is the law of God or the will of God. He now believes that it is the will of God *for him personally.* Nor does he believe that this will of God has been revealed to him only that he might see how far away from God he is, how sinful he is.

Not at all; he believes in all earnestness that God through the Word and his conscience has revealed His will *that he should do it,* do it every day and in all things.

This is the heroic aspect of his faith!

And doubly heroic, because the awakened soul through innumerable defeats has been given to feel that it is impossible for him to do this. Day after day he has experienced the impossibility of so doing.

And still he believes in the law of God! Believes that it is God's will that he should keep it, not only learn it, speak of it, think about it, be humbled by it, and desire its fulfilment.

His conscience, which has now been enlightened by the Word of God, says, "Thou shalt!" And he believes the Word of God speaking to him through his conscience.

*

This is doubly remarkable in our day, because most preachers who still preach the law of God take the edge off the sword of the law at the very moment when the law is about to strike the sinner.

They speak clearly and forcibly about what the law of God requires.

But no sooner have they done this than they hasten to say to the awakened soul which has begun to take these divine requirements seriously and is therefore ready to proceed to fulfil them: This, you understand, is the law and the will of God. And you and I must know what the law of God is. But you must not imagine that you can fulfil it. For that you cannot do. And to think that you can is only a manifestation of the self-confidence and pride which is inherent in your old nature. You should much rather thank God that Christ has fulfilled the law in your stead, and that you need only believe on Him to be saved.

This way of dealing with such souls is unquestionably the usual one in our day. Moreover, it is motivated by a sincere concern for these awakened souls. Those who thus deal with such souls desire to help them not to come *under the law,* but to lay hold of grace and become free and happy Christians at once.

Their intentions are undoubtedly good, but the result of such cure of souls is not good.

Here truth and falsehood are blended together in an unfortunate manner. It is true that Christ has fulfilled the law in our stead. It is true that we need only believe on Christ to be saved.

But, they forget that a soul cannot believe on Christ until he has been made to feel his own helplessness. They have forgotten the words of the apostle that by the *law* cometh the knowledge of sin (Romans 3:20). They have forgotten that God *killeth* before He maketh alive (I Samuel 2:6). And that it is by the law that He killeth (Galatians 2:19). They have forgotten that man is killed by the law only as he fulfils it. "When the commandment came, sin revived, and I died," says the apostle (Romans 7:9).

With their good intentions they would exempt the awakened soul from laboring under the law, in order forthwith to enable him to believe in the grace of God. But as a result of this the believing soul believes neither in the law nor in grace. For he appropriates the grace of God with his head only and not with his heart, as is the case with such a disagreeably large number of souls in the extremely *evangelical* age in which we are living.

In times past, when people were more legalistic, there were no doubt many more believers who had really been made free in Christ than there are in our day. For the simple reason that men had been "killed" by the law and therefore felt the need of the Gospel, whereby they also acquired the inner qualifications for *believing* in the Gospel, not merely knowing it.

In this connection I am reminded of the boy who wanted to help the butterfly out of its pupa.

He saw that it struggled hard to get loose. Only a few strands held it back. So the boy clipped these off. The butterfly was free. And the boy was very happy both about the butterfly and about the little operation he had performed. But so much greater did his sorrow become when he discovered what a well-intended but destructive labor of love he had performed. The butterfly could not fly and could not learn to fly. The exertions by which it was to have worked itself out of the pupa were what would have enabled it to fly.

In our day we have many such awakened souls in our midst.

By premature midwifery they have been helped past those birth-throes which are the necessary conditions for giving birth to life.

But should we not preach the Gospel to the awakened souls then, some will ask.

Indeed, we should.

But we should preach both law and Gospel, both sin and salvation. Awakened souls should hear about the grace of God in Christ, and in every sermon. But we should not in mistaken zeal and in impatience interfere prematurely.

We must give both *law* and *grace* time and opportunity to work in the awakened soul, and help him to believe in both.

And never try to make ourselves believe that we can persuade any one to believe in the Gospel before we by the grace of God have helped him to believe in the law of God, the will of God.

And note well, to believe that they must *do* the will of God.

Not until then will they have tested their own strength, and because of the unyielding requirements of their new born conscience become so worn out and exhausted that they know of nothing else to do but to give up at the very foot of the cross of Christ. Not until then do they "learn" to believe in the Gospel.

No one can learn this merely by acquiring the theory of it. This can only be learned in life, in life's bitter struggle with the law of God, when the soul has been "killed" by the law. And experiences that *that* is the way to life in the Son of God.

Conscience and Our Old Nature

"For I through the law died unto the law, that I might live unto God."
—GALATIANS 2:19.

CONSCIENCE says to the awakened soul: Thou shalt love thy God above all else, and thy neighbor as thyself.

The daily experiences of life tell him, however, that this is impossible.

But he still believes his conscience, and, undaunted, tries over and over again to do as his conscience bids him.

He does not give up. Nor does he lower the requirements until it is possible for him to meet them. Not at all; he believes in the justice of God's demands and that God has the right to require these things of him.

But, obviously, a situation such as this drives an awakened soul to utter *despair*.

What will become of him, unable as he is to become any different from what he is? Others succeed in so doing. They find peace with God. But to him this seems impossible.

At this point some might ask: But does he not know anything about the grace of God?

Yes, he does. He has heard about it in sermon after sermon. He has read about it in his Bible day after day. And Christian friends have spoken to him about it in quiet hours that they have spent together.

Here we see what a mysterious thing the Word of God is.

It is a two-edged sword, the Bible says.

The law is in the Gospel and the Gospel in the law.

All depends upon the ears with which you hear the Word.

The ears of an awakened and repentant sinner hear the law even in the most glorious promises of grace. Such a soul says to himself, "These things are all true. God is gracious. Verily He has wrought a wondrous salvation through His Son."

But what good does all this do me?

Even though God were again as merciful as He is, yea, even if it were possible to imagine that Jesus might sacrifice Himself once again for sinners, still He could not help me.

For to do so would not be moral on His part.

Regardless of how merciful He is, He cannot forgive a sinner who does not sufficiently regret his sins, who is *divided* in heart and half-willed, who, in fact, *loves* sin.

It is not difficult to see that nothing seems to condemn such a person more than the grace of God. He says to himself, "Here you can see in what a terrible condition I am. God is good and gracious, but I am so wicked that not even a God as merciful as He is can do anything with a person like me."

The more such a soul as this through the increasingly pointed demands of his conscience feels the hardness of his own heart, his indifference, his coolness, and his carelessness, the more he is driven to the thought that the Spirit of God has forsaken him. It makes him inwardly burned out so to speak. He thinks that he has committed the unpardonable sin spoken of in the Scriptures. It is the easier for him to think so because he feels that it is more terrible **no**w than it ever was to act contrary to his conscience.

Before his awakening he had, to be sure, felt some degree of anxiety whenever he had permitted the admon-

ishing voice of his conscience to go unheeded. But this is
entirely different. Now he errs every day, in thought,
word, and deed. And the terrible thing about it is that he
is nearly always fully aware of what he is doing. Conscience cries out with a strong and authoritative voice:
Thou shalt not! But he does it nevertheless, and afterwards experiences a paralyzing fear. He is destroying
something within himself, in fact the holiest and most
precious thing he has.

In Hebrews 10:26 we read that those who commit the
sin which is unto death "sin wilfully." And now this soul
says to himself, "That is what I am doing. The sins which
I committed before my awakening were comparatively innocent, because then my conscience did not speak to me as
clearly and authoritatively as it does now."

However, he himself furnishes the best proof every day
that he has *not* committed the unpardonable sin: His
thoughts center constantly in Christ and His cross.
He thinks of nothing else, and there is nothing that he so
earnestly desires as to secure forgiveness for all his sins
and be at peace with God.

The most certain proof of all that he has not committed
this sin is that he cries to God continually about his *sins*.
He also *confesses* his sins, over and over again. If he
could, he would turn his heart inside out before God in
order to be certain that there was no self-deception or dishonesty anywhere.

Behold, such is the heart which is "perfect toward the
Lord!"

*

It is not easy to exercise the right kind of cure of souls
when ministering to people of this type. Oftentimes they
are dealt with rather harshly and unsympathetically.

I am not thinking now of the type of monstrosity which
the leader of a spiritual awakening in a certain community

perpetrated. An awakened soul came to him one evening after the meeting and complained of his condition, seeking help and counsel. To which the leader replied, "What is the matter with you anyway? Didn't we pray for you several days ago?" This is, fortunately, an exception. But this was actually said by the leader of a spiritual movement, a statement which revealed, of course, not only a complete lack of understanding, but of sympathy as well.

But even where a leader sympathizes sincerely with the trials and struggles of the awakened soul, there can still be not a little lack of understanding of the distress which I have pictured above.

Some preachers think that it is because these people are ignorant of the Gospel that they do not attain peace and assurance, and for that reason they think that all these souls need is *instruction*. It is true, of course, that definite knowledge of the mystery of the Gospel is needed. We shall say more about that later. But it is my belief that we shall not be able to *apply* this knowledge in such a way as to be of real help to these people until we realize that it is their *conscience* which is making it difficult for them to believe. It is their conscience which forbids them to believe, to accept the grace which God proffers them in the Word of Christ.

Especially must we be on guard lest we misunderstand the protest of their conscience, and look upon it as a sort of contrariness or self-wilfulness on the part of these seeking souls when they do not submit to the plain message of the Gospel and do not rest in what the Word of God says.

The temptation to do so is not very far removed when we have spoken to the person concerned a large number of times and have heard the same objections each time. Such people will make the most ingenious attempts to show that certain passages of the Bible cannot be interpreted as simply and directly as we think. They will call our attention again and again to obscure words and sayings in the Bible which seem to limit and circumscribe its plain promises concerning the grace of God.

Then it is important to *understand*.

To understand that it is *conscience* that is back of all this ingenious thinking and argumentation. To understand that conscience is afraid of deceiving itself, afraid of appropriating the grace of God with the intellect through a dead faith and not receiving it into the heart.

This fear in the heart of a seeking soul we should never seek to quench. It is sound and fruitful, and should never be extinguished. The important thing is to understand how to make use of it properly and direct it into right channels. But more about this later.

*

We have now tried to show how an awakened conscience *functions,* as experienced by an awakened and repentant sinner.

Now we shall try to show what God has sought to accomplish through these experiences.

We shall begin by underscoring that "all these things are of God." He has planned it all. He it is, too, who has been fulfilling it. All the way. There is, then, a divine *plan*, and it is that which we would now seek to find and follow.

A clear and profound statement of this plan occurs early in Old Testament times, in Hannah's simple words, "Jehovah *killeth* and maketh alive" (I Samuel 2:6).

A killing process is here taking place, one which is being carried out under the direction of the Lord. Jesus, too, has made mention of this putting to death, "Whosoever shall lose his life shall preserve it" (Luke 17:33).

The Apostle Paul also speaks of this death and this killing process: "I was alive apart from the law once; but when the commandment came, sin revived, and I *died;* and the commandment, which was unto life, this I found to be *unto death"* (Romans 7:9-10). "For I *through the law died* unto the law, that I might live unto God" (Galatians 2:19).

These Biblical truths have now for some time all but disappeared from our preaching.

We have limited ourselves to one or two passages dealing with the law, such as these: "through the law cometh the knowledge of sin" (Romans 3:20) and "the law is become our tutor to bring us unto Christ, that we might be justified by faith" (Galatians 3:24).

We have confined ourselves largely to these two passages, and thought that the function of the law was only to produce the knowledge of sin and thus drive the sinner to Christ. And we have passed by in silence Paul's words about the *killing* work of the *law.* While we have not said anything against it, neither have we said anything for it.

But our preaching has suffered as a result.

We have been called to preach "the whole counsel of God." And if we do not do so, there will be things in the experience of our listeners which will not be properly clarified by the Word, and which will therefore be a hindrance to the sound development of their life in God. That this has actually taken place has become exceedingly apparent.

If I understand the situation correctly, there is in our day an exceptionally large number of people who have been awakened and who are repentant, but who do not have peace and assurance. Many of them continue in this state for a long time, frequently to the accompaniment of much spiritual distress.

I have a conviction that it is more difficult for the preaching of our day to help these people than anybody else.

The reason for this is, no doubt, that we do not understand these people as well as we do the others. They are just a little outside the pale of those ordinary rubrics for the cure of souls which we have formulated to our own satisfaction with such comparative ease.

These folk would undoubtedly receive more help from us than they do if we were better qualified to preach and if we spoke more about what the Scriptures call the *killing* work of the law.

They would receive an answer to the question that is constantly annoying them: Why does God deal with me as He does? Why does He not give me peace and assurance?

Why is He so harsh in His dealings with me?

There is nothing that I would rather do than believe in His grace alone.

This question becomes particularly annoying, in fact, almost unendurable, when this inner distress increases and turns into anxiety and despair. Why is God so *severe?*

Why does He strike so *violently?*

This question the Bible answers very simply by saying: He *killeth.*

There is something within us that must be put to death. And that something God deliberately kills, whether we understand what He is doing or not.

Nor does He ask us preachers for permission thus to kill.

What is it then that must be put to death?

"*I* died," says the Apostle.

It is the old *I* which must be put to death. Our self-

life must be bruised and broken. And not our self-life
in the form of egoism and self-wilfulness only. That too.
But what we wish to emphasize here first and foremost
is that our ethical life in its relation to God must be brok-
en. It is that confidence which I have in myself, in my
own understanding of spiritual things, in my own will, in
my own religion and morality, that confidence in myself
with which I always oppose God and which is the real
hindrance to my being saved, which must be broken.

To break our own inherent and deeply rooted self-confidence, which is fallen man's deepest hurt, is undoubtedly
the most difficult work that God has to accomplish within
us.

And when we see how He does it, we must stand before Him in awe, adoration, and thanksgiving.

He breaks our old self-life.

This He does by driving it to exhaustion, to a point
where it has spent all its energies and lies at His feet,
surrendered and brought to naught—killed.

And this He does by the help of conscience, after it
has been enlightened by the Word of God and born anew
by a spiritual awakening.

This driving to death takes place by various stages,
so to speak, in which God by the help of conscience
steadily makes life harder and more difficult for our old
nature.

Let us now consider this a little more closely. It will
be similar to following the course of a spiritual awakening
anew, but from a different angle.

*

An ordinary natural man, who lives as folk usually do,
would not deny that he has failings and shortcomings,
that he is not as religious as he should be, and that there
are also certain defects in his moral life.

But with respect to his own old nature he is still very optimistic.

He will alter and improve it when the time comes, but for the present things are not propitious for making the necessary changes in his manner of living.

Then God brings all this to naught.

Through the Word and a conscience which has been made sensitive by a spiritual awakening this man begins to see that what he needs is repentance and an entirely new life.

But his old self-life is not broken by this.

He reasons now that his great and important task is to repent, and this he sets about to accomplish in all earnestness. Heretofore he has lived thoughtlessly and frivolously; now he has determined that there is to be a change; he has decided to repent.

But then God spoils his plans in this respect also.

Through the Word of God and an awakened conscience this man begins to realize that repentance is something vastly different from what he at first thought it was. He begins to understand that repentance involves a *change of heart*.

But neither is his old nature brought to naught by this.

He starts in again, and applies himself more diligently than ever. He prays God every day for a new attitude of heart. He tries to have fellowship with God in the Word and in holy meditation. He associates a great deal with Christian people. Above all, he struggles against his sins, not only in word and deed, but also in thought, desire, and imagination. He does not succeed very well, it is true, but his old self does not give up hope nevertheless. He will be more successful later, he thinks, after he has had a little more practice in being God-fearing and holy.

But then God breaks this up also.

Through the Word and his sensitive conscience the awakened soul begins to see that the attitude God expects him to have is one of *love*. And, peculiarly enough, to *love* God is the only thing he cannot do. Aside from that he can do not a little. He can pray earnestly to God. He can hear and read the Word reverently and with devotion. He can forsake sin and ungodliness. He can serve God by sacrificing time, effort, and money for Him and His cause. He can even suffer a little for the sake of the name of Christ. But he cannot succeed in making himself love God. For his conscience says quietly but authoritatively: It is not for His sake you are doing all this, but for your own. Now as before you love yourself above all else.

Nor is his old self brought to naught by this.

He still has a way out. Strange that he did not make use of it before. That way is the way of contrition.

The Bible relates in a very impressive way how willing God is to accept a contrite soul. Accordingly, he now begins to repent and confess. Do not all the preachers say, too, that all that is necessary in order to be saved is to come to God as a contrite sinner, and receive forgiveness for the sake of Jesus Christ?

But now God spoils this also.

Through the Word and his sensitive conscience the awakened soul begins to see that his contrition is just as self-centered as all the other things he has set out to do. He can be sorry for his sins after a fashion. But he is not sorry because he sins against God and grieves His loving heart. By no means, he is sorry, as all egoists are, because of the unfortunate consequences of sin. Were it not for that, his heart would be as cold as ice and as hard as stone. He *sees* plainly enough that he sins against God every day, but it does not *grieve* him.

Nor is his old self brought to naught by this.

But there is still another way out. And it is more than strange that he has not seen it before. This way is the way of *faith*. Does not the whole New Testament proclaim the fact that in the new dispensation a sinner is saved by grace? By grace alone. The preachers all explain this thoroughly and make it very plain: Only believe!

The awakened soul now tries to believe in all earnestness. And now he thinks that everything will be all right, for it is only necessary to believe. That is all!

But then God brings to naught this also.

For it becomes plain to his awakened conscience that it is not so easy to believe as he thought it would be. Only believe! There is more to this than "only," says the honest seeker.

At last he too, most likely, comes to the conclusion that he knows of nothing as difficult as to believe.

He has no trouble, of course, in believing what the Scriptures say about the grace of God, about Christ's vicarious atonement, and about justification by faith alone. But how is he to believe that all this was for him? Not that he has committed more or bigger sins than other people. But how can God forgive a sinner who is not sorry at heart for his sins, but who on the contrary secretly clings to sin instead of hating it?

*

At last it has been accomplished.

God has "killed" the old self. It is worn out, exhausted. It has tried *everything,* everything of which it has heard and everything that it has been able to devise by itself.

And each time it thought that it could save itself. But now it sees no further way out; and glimpses, therefore, not a single possibility of being saved.

This is what Søren Kierkegaard calls "the absolute self-despair."

Such a person has lost confidence in himself—wholly and completely. And therefore also thinks that he is eternally lost. For he has been relying on himself all the time, upon himself alone. And when he now, as the result of an awakened conscience, is compelled to give up hope in himself, he thinks, in all seriousness, that he is hopelessly lost. If he could not save himself by one of the methods described above, certainly there is no one else that can save him.

The Scriptures say something about God's purpose with the commandment being to "make sin *exceeding sinful*" (Romans 7:13). And: "that what the law saith, it speaketh that *every mouth* may be *stopped,* and all the world may be brought under the judgment of God."

This is what has now taken place in the sinner's life.

Without himself knowing it. He thinks that the whole thing has failed. In his opinion his whole awakening and conversion, which began so well, has been completely ruined. And in such a way that no one, neither God nor himself, can resurrect it.

God has now accomplished what He desired by this killing, by this hard, painful, and fearful process of putting to death.

What was it, then, that He desired?

Paul expresses it thus in one place, "So the law is become our tutor to bring us to Christ" (Galatians 3:24). This soul has now been tutored to come to Christ.

And it is his conscience, his conscience new-born

through the Word and his spiritual awakening, that God has used to tutor the sinner to Christ.

The sinner himself, however, does not understand this.

He himself thinks that he has never been as far away from Christ as he is now.

But his daily life is the best proof of the fact that he is mistaken. For as a matter of fact his thoughts and longings center in nothing else all the day long than in Christ and His cross, even when he thinks that God has cast him away and that he is therefore irretrievably lost.

*

Let us here take note of the situation in which the seeking soul now finds himself.

God has succeeded, through His Word and an awakened conscience, in telling him the whole truth about himself. And now the sinner believes this truth in its entirety.

But at the same time God has been able through His Word and a sensitive conscience to declare unto him the truth of the Gospel, the truth about the finished work of Christ, and all that God in mercy has done for the salvation of sinners.

All this the sinner now believes.

Without himself knowing it he has come into possession of a faith in God's *law* and in God's *grace* which is touching and impressive.

There is only this difficulty, that this faith does not give the man himself any rest and peace. He has been tutored to Christ, and he is not satisfied to be anywhere else but at the cross of Christ.

However, there is this about it: he cannot find *rest* there either.

He believes in Christ, but he doubts himself.

And he does both so completely that he thinks it is impossible for him to become a participant in God's salvation. He believes in the grace of God, in the finished atonement wrought by Christ, and in His willingness to forgive sins. But he does not dare to appropriate any of it unto himself.

There are two reasons for this, which in reality are only one. Let us, however, for the sake of perspective, divide it into two.

In the first place, this soul has not really grasped that which God has had in mind to teach him through all this, namely: Your old life and your old self are so thoroughly depraved that you cannot change or improve them. Having shown you this, there is only one thing for you to do and that is to acknowledge that that is what you are, and that you yourself cannot alter your old self-life. All you need to do is to come with your incurable self and lay it down at the foot of my cross. There you will receive, first of all, forgiveness for the fact that you are evil throughout, and thereupon I will create a new personality within you.

But this is the very thing to which the seeking soul finds it so difficult to accede.

He thinks quite instinctively, on the basis of his old nature's inherent view of these things, that it is *through his conscience* that he is to be changed, that it is his conscience which is to produce the change, the moral and religious change, within him.

That is why his despair becomes so great when he discovers that he himself is unable to effect a change in his old attitude of heart.

In the second place, it is equally difficult for the awakened soul to grasp that which God would teach him about forgiveness. That God forgives is, as already stated, not difficult for him to believe. The difficulty centers rather in *how* God forgives.

The *basis* of forgiveness, is what is hard for him to understand.

Here again he experiences no difficulty in believing that the atoning death of Christ is the basis. The difficulty lies in believing that it is *only* for Christ's sake that forgiveness is imparted.

It is in this connection that his conscience becomes disquieted.

Can God *for Jesus' sake* forgive a person who cannot separate himself from his old sins? Is it not written, "repent and believe the Gospel" (Mark 1:15)? It is in repenting that I fail. Has a man a right to believe in the Gospel when he has not rightly repented of his sins?

Furthermore: Can God *for Jesus' sake* forgive a man who in his *heart clings* to sin? Do not the Scriptures speak of those whose hearts are perfect toward the Lord?

Again: Can God *for Jesus' sake* forgive a person who does not believe, who only doubts and fears? Is it not written that "without faith it is impossible to be well-pleasing unto him" (Hebrews 11:6)?

*

These are the difficulties which a seeking soul encounters in believing in forgiveness.

They constitute an old problem.

Paul refers to it when he speaks of the righteousness of the *law* and the righteousness of *faith,* of being saved by the law and of being saved by faith.

To be saved by the law is our old nature's way of being saved.

We believe instinctively that God cannot love us and forgive us unless He can find something *good* within us.

To begin with we all think that there *is* something good within us. And we think that God will forgive us when He sees this.

Afterwards we begin to realize that there is nothing good within us. Thereupon we try to *become* good, to change our manner of living and our attitude of heart. Then we think that when God sees this He will have mercy upon us.

Later we begin to see that in us dwelleth no good thing; furthermore, that we cannot bring forth anything good from within ourselves. Then we begin to think that *God* must *work* something good within us: a new attitude of heart, real sorrow for sin, power to be victorious over sin, and so forth. And then we think that when God sees this He will be in a position to forgive us our sins and make us His children.

Conscience and Grace

"If our heart condemn us, God is greater than our heart, and knoweth all things."
—I JOHN 3:20.

OUR old nature misunderstands the *salvation* of God in a twofold way.

First, it believes that salvation is through the law, that is, through the conscience, that the law through the conscience must make man well-pleasing in the sight of God.

When it has become convinced that this is impossible, then it believes that it can receive *knowledge* of God's wondrous salvation *from conscience.*

Both conceptions are fundamentally erroneous, and bear testimony to the innate confidence that we have in ourselves, and of how we turn this self-confidence *against* God.

Left to himself man would know nothing about salvation, nor would his conscience. Not even a conscience made alert by a spiritual awakening can impart to man knowledge of the salvation of God.

It is a *"mystery,"* the Scriptures say—a mystery of God.

"Let a man so account of us, as of ministers of Christ, and stewards of the *mysteries* of God" (I Corinthians 4:1).

"Making known unto us the *mystery* of his will, according to his good pleasure which he purposed in him" (Ephesians 1:9).

"Whereby, when ye read, ye can perceive my understanding in the *mystery* of Christ" (Ephesians 3:4).

"Praying at all seasons . . . , and on my behalf, that utterance may be given unto me in opening my mouth, to make known with boldness the *mystery* of the Gospel" (Ephesians 6:19).

We human beings receive knowledge of this mystery only as God *reveals* it: "Now to him that is able to establish you according to my Gospel and the preaching of Jesus Christ, according to the revelation of the mystery which hath been kept in silence through times eternal, but now is manifested, and by the scriptures of the prophets, according to the commandment of the eternal God, is made known unto all the nations unto obedience of faith" (Romans 16:25-26).

What, then, is this mystery of God concerning salvation?

The simplest answer to this question is undoubtedly the one found in Romans 3:21: "But now *apart from the law* a righteousness hath been manifested, being witnessed by the law and the prophets: even the righteousness of God *through faith* in Jesus Christ unto all them that believe."

And the most mysterious aspect of this mystery is the one of which we read in the following: "But to him that worketh not, but believeth on him that justifieth the ungodly, his faith is reckoned for righteousness" (Romans 4:5).

Here God reveals the mystery that He justifies or forgives *him that worketh not,* that is, him who is not able to do what the law through an awakened conscience requires.

"The ungodly!" it says, in order to obviate all misunderstanding. And is it not ungodly in the deepest sense of the word that the awakened soul feels that he is?

The ungodly, God says, in order to reveal to us the mystery that He loves us and forgives us even though there is nothing *within us* to warrant His doing so.

But conscience protests and continues its accusations.

And this is perfectly in order. That is what it is supposed to do. God Himself has appointed it as a public accuser. Its duty is to point out everything of which the sinner is guilty and which deserves to be punished.

But the accuser has no right to interfere in the *granting of pardon.*

Salvation consists in God granting pardon to the guilty, even to such as are guilty of the penalty of death.

The Biblical expression "to justify" really means to pardon, to remit the penalty of the guilty.

"Who shall lay anything to the charge of God's elect? It is God that justifieth; who is he that condemneth? It is Christ Jesus that died, yea rather, that was raised from the dead, who is at the right hand of God, who also maketh intercession for us" (Romans 8:33-34).

*

But conscience objects again. Is not this to judge unrighteously? Was it not this that the ancient prophets reproved so strongly in the judges of Israel, that they acquitted the guilty and imposed sentence that the innocent should suffer?

Of a truth, we do not lack boldness! We even dare to question whether God deals righteously or not!

What right have we to question Him? As though we knew better what righteousness is than the holy and righteous God Himself.

Nay; if God does a thing, it *is* right.

Should not that be enough for us, insignificant children of men that we are!

But listen. So gracious is our righteous God that He has even tried to explain to us that He is not unrighteous when He acquits the ungodly.

He says, "Whom God set forth to be a propitiation, through faith, in his blood, to show his righteousness because of the passing over of the sins done aforetime, in the forbearance of God; for the showing, I say, of his righteousness at this present season: that he might himself *be* just, and the *justifier* of him that hath faith in Jesus" (Romans 3:25-26).

Here we are told how He could be just and at the same time justify the ungodly. The righteous punishment due us because of sin God took upon Himself when He in the Son became one with the human race and as our Substitute bore the guilt and punishment of sin: "Him who knew no sin he made to be sin on our behalf; that we might become the righteousness of God in him" (II Corinthians 5:21). "He was wounded for our transgressions, he was bruised for our iniquities; the chastisement of our peace was upon him; and with his stripes we are healed" (Isaiah 53:5).

This is the *reason* why God loves us, and the only reason.

In us there are no grounds for being loved and forgiven. Nor is this necessary, for Jesus is my Substitute. And since God's own Son has made my cause His own, I can be at peace. He says, too, "My grace is sufficient for thee" (II Corinthians 12:9).

If, meanwhile, any of my readers should say, "Well, that is the way God has explained the mystery of the atonement; but, nevertheless, I do not understand it," then I would reply, "Nor do I!"

And you and I, my dear reader, should thank God
that He does not expect us to understand either Him
or the mystery of His salvation. He has only asked us
to *believe* on Him. Most of us cannot explain why the
sun shines either.

Nor is it necessary. It sheds its rays upon us whether
we understand it or not, if we will only walk in its light.

Let me here call attention to the incident of the Israelites being bitten by fiery serpents.

Israel had again been rebellious and disobedient. As
we read of their disobedience it seems to us that it exceed-
ed all bounds. But let us be careful in passing judgment.
Israel's sins were all enumerated. Imagine if our daily
life should be kept account of in the same meticulous way!
What a record of disobedience and rebelliousness it would
be.

As we said, Israel had been disobedient again. And
this time the Lord punished them very severely. He sent
exceedingly poisonous serpents into their camp. People
died like flies from the poisonous bites of the reptiles.

Then the people cried with repentant hearts unto the
Lord. And He helped them this time also. But in a
quite original way. He desired to help them, not only
against the serpents, but also against their unbelief. He
would exercise them in faith. So He caused Moses to
set a serpent of brass upon a standard in the midst of the
camp, and then told the people that those who had been
bitten need only look unto the serpent of brass and they
would be healed immediately.

Did the Israelites understand this?

Certainly not, and there were unquestionably some
who doubted—and perished.

But those who looked unto the serpent of brass were

saved. They had only the *Word of God* upon which to depend. Their distress, however, was so great that it impelled them to avail themselves of the provision made by God for their healing. And they found that it was sufficient.

"And as Moses lifted up the serpent in the wilderness, even so must the Son of man be lifted up; that whosoever believeth may in him have eternal life" (John 3:14-15).

As Israel in the wilderness, so we, too, are doomed to perish. The serpent's poison is in us, in our soul and in our body. But to look to the cross is sufficient for doomed sinners!

Is there any one who understands this? No. And for that reason many doubt and deny it.

But they who look unto the Lamb of God who taketh away the sins of the world are quickened unto life. Every one. And that immediately! Also those who are afraid, and who are distressed by uncertainty and doubt, and who are aware that the poison is still working within them. They are saved, even though they do not realize it as yet. For salvation does not depend upon our *knowing* that we are saved any more than it depends upon our *understanding* it. It depends only upon our *looking* unto the Lamb of God in our distress.

The serpent's poison has penetrated into every part of my being.

But I am in no danger whatsoever. Mine is the serpent of brass! And whosoever believeth shall in Him have eternal life.

I need but be ungodly. Salvation is in my Saviour. But He cannot impart this salvation to me until I see that I have been bitten unto death.

And this I have been given to see through the law, and through a conscience which has been born anew.

Conscience and Faith

"Let us draw near with a true heart in fulness of faith, having our hearts sprinkled from an evil conscience."

—HEBREWS 10:22.

"WITH the heart man believeth," says the apostle in Romans 10:10.

We have seen that "heart" is used both in the Old and in the New Testament where conscience is sometimes meant. Whether the apostle uses it here in that sense or not, I do not know. But whether he uses it here in the ordinary Biblical sense in which heart is used, that is, as the spiritual center of man's life, or whether he means conscience, is immaterial. For the heart includes, obviously, also conscience. And even though heart in the ordinary sense of the word includes more than conscience, it is nevertheless clear, after our previous inquiry, that the central thing in the heart is conscience.

For, as we observed above, conscience is not merely that self-consciousness which is peculiar to man. At the same time as it is this, it is consciousness of himself in relation to God; which is the same as saying that conscience is the vital link between man's *self*-consciousness and his *God*-consciousness.

The apostle's words were, "with the heart man believeth."

After what we have said above, we might even dare to restate them thus: "with the conscience man believeth."

Moreover, this is true of all types of faith in God, not only *Christian,* but *pagan* as well. No man possesses any other faith in God than that which springs forth from the immediate assurance of his own conscience.

A person can, it is true, without any connection with conscience whatsoever, have *knowledge* of God, *longing* after God, *consciousness* of God, or *fantasies* and *dreams* about God. But we do not look upon a man's God-consciousness as faith in God unless it occupies the central and leading place in his personality and exercises the determining influence upon his will.

In the latter event it is clear that faith is a fruit of conscience. For it is his conscience which gives his consciousness of God the leading place in his personality. Likewise it is his conscience which by its categorical imperative gives his God-consciousness power over his will.

We can now say that the heathen's faith in God consists in his will submitting to that consciousness of God and the divine will which his conscience intuitively makes known to him.

*

Turning now to the Christian's faith in God, it is comparatively clear, after our previous inquiry, that his faith is a fruit of the new-creation of conscience which the miracle of spiritual awakening performs in his soul.

Through the Word and the new-born conscience God makes known His will to sinful man. Then the sinner must choose, whether to submit to the categorical and absolute judgment of his conscience, or, in rebelliousness and dissimulation, seek to evade the judgment of his conscience.

If he chooses to submit, *faith* is born within him.

That choice is the first act of faith. He believes in that law of God with which he has become acquainted through the Word and which through his conscience passes its sentence of death upon him.

The fact that he believes in this law, even though through his conscience it pronounces his death sentence, can be accounted for solely by the fact that he feels that it is the judgment of *God* upon him.

Had he not felt that it was the judgment of God, he would never have accepted it, because it seems so unreasonable from an intellectual viewpoint.

We can therefore truthfully say that any one who through an awakened conscience believes in the law of God, believes in God also.

He believes that it is *God* who speaks to him.

Let us pay particular attention to this. For faith is in reality and in its deepest essence to believe in God because it is *God* who speaks, and not because what He says is self-evident or intelligible.

Let us further note that faith in its deepest essence and in its most mysterious aspect is linked with conscience. This is because faith arises through the *conscience* and not through the *intellect*.

Our intellect convinces us only of those things which are self-evident and intelligible. In thinking, everything depends upon the *reasons* advanced, upon the *arguments* put forth.

Conscience, on the other hand, never gives reasons for its judgments, as we have noted above. It simply *gives expression* to its judgments, categorically, absolutely, and without subject to appeal. It brings us face to face with the will of God, which needs no supporting reason besides the fact that it is the will of God, which is just what conscience assures us it is.

*

As soon as an awakened soul believes in the law of God, even though it condemns him, he has entered into faith's true and normal relationship with God, a relationship which can be expressed most clearly and profoundly in the words which the youthful Samuel learned of the aged servant of the Lord: "Speak, Lord; for thy servant heareth" (I Samuel 3:9).

God can now therefore also begin to preach the *Gospel* to this soul. The awakened soul which has begun to believe in the paradoxical law of God has also, by so doing, made it possible for himself to believe in the paradoxical grace of God.

This accounts for a fact which we have frequently observed, that skeptics and atheists, once having permitted themselves to be condemned and made humble by the moral demands of Christianity, afterwards have experienced no great difficulty in believing the same Gospel which they formerly rejected because of the great intellectual difficulties involved.

Have these people, then, finally mastered all these difficulties? Indeed not. But through their new-born conscience they have entered into a relationship with God in which all they need to do is to hear *God* speak, and they submit from their own free inner conviction, whether that which God says is intelligible to them or not.

As the Gospel is then preached to the awakened soul, who now by believing in the law of God has received new ears with which to hear the Gospel, we see how faith in the grace of God begins to grow.

He believes in a childlike, direct way everything that the Scriptures proclaim about our gracious God and Father: about His unfathomable love toward sinners; His incarnation, suffering, and death for the sins of man; about justification by faith, prayer, and answer to prayer; about His gracious leading of the individual and of the nations; and about eternal heaven and eternal hell.

But, as we have noted above, his great difficulty, especially to begin with, is that he does not dare to appropriate this *unto himself*.

This is not because he has any doubts about the Bible or about God. On the contrary, it is himself he doubts. He doubts himself so completely and has such lack of confidence in himself that it is impossible for him to believe that God's salvation is for him also.

He is so humble before God and so reverent toward Him that he does not dare to believe in the forgiveness of sins. He feels that it is incompatible with the moral nature of God to forgive a sinner who neither regrets his sins sufficiently, as he thinks, nor has been wholly separated from them.

Many would condemn this as unbelief. But that is an injustice. We can say that it is an incomplete faith. But it certainly is not unbelief.

In the first place, we do not find here a trace of that taking offense at God which is so characteristic of unbelief. On the contrary, this sinner acquiesces in what God says. As a matter of fact, he even thinks that it would be right of God not to be able to receive him and forgive him.

In the second place, we notice that this sinner does not run away from God, which would be the natural thing for him to do all the while that he himself thinks that he is so constituted that God cannot forgive him. If it were unbelief on his part, he would, of course, turn away from God, either in rebelliousness or in indifference. But instead of this we note that his whole being centers in God day and night, his longings, his thoughts, his prayers, and even his sins.

Is not this to believe?

Yea, verily. One might be almost tempted to ask: Can God find anywhere a faith that is greater than this very despairing faith itself, a faith which feels that everything is militating against it and which feels that it does not possess a single ray of light in the midst of all its darkness, but which, notwithstanding all this, does not take offense at God, but believes that God is right in all that He does?

*

Many are of the opinion, nevertheless, that something is lacking in the faith of this seeking soul, that there is something about which he is mistaken. He should believe, they say, when God says, "I justify the ungodly."

Of course, there is *some* truth in this. But I do not think that it is entirely correct. I believe that we may say that the faith of such seeking souls is *incomplete,* but not *erroneous.*

Faith is a paradoxical thing.

It has more aspects than many are willing to see. In the Scriptures it is placed in opposition to *works.* But that is the very thing we are tempted to do, make faith a matter of works. It is inherent in our fallen nature to do so.

The Catholics have done this in a very *gross* manner.

We Protestants sometimes do the same thing, but in a *finer* way: Faith is a gift of God, and is, therefore, not a meritorious act on our part. But it is, nevertheless, the act whereby the sinner at last saves himself from perdition, after having tried all other ways and found them hopeless.

There is, obviously, an element of truth in this. But the whole matter becomes all wrong unless we take into account another aspect of faith, one which the Scriptures emphasize.

This aspect I find most clearly expressed in the words of Jesus, "Whosoever shall not receive the kingdom of

God as a little child, he shall in no wise enter therein"
(Mark 10:15).

How does a *little* child receive the kingdom of God?

This is in truth one of the most exceedingly profound
mysteries of the Gospel. The little child does nothing,
cannot do anything, can neither pray nor read nor repent
nor abstain from innate sin. But neither does the child
put forth any opposition. It does not hinder God from
saving it.

And *therefore* the child is saved—for that reason, and
for no other.

For God *wills* that all men should be saved, and He
saves all who do not put forth any opposition to His salvation.

The little child does not belong only to Adam's fallen
race; he belongs also that race which has been given
its second Adam, man's Substitute, who on behalf of the
race has atoned for the sin of the race.

According to the New Testament God has obligated
Himself to give every member of the race a part in this
salvation. This He does upon His own initiative. He
does not wait until the sinner asks Him to do so. Before
the sinner begins to pray for salvation, the most essential
and most difficult part of salvation has already been accomplished from God's side.

We adults must receive the kingdom of God as the
little children do, Jesus says.

And He says, further, that we must *repent* in order to
become as children (Matthew 18:3).

This tells us what the real significance of repentance
and faith is in connection with our salvation. Through
repentance and faith we are to become what the little
child already is, one who puts forth no opposition to

God. That is why it is saved. For it is God who accomplished our whole salvation.

We are now deep into the most paradoxical aspect of faith.

To believe is not to save my soul by "laying hold" of Christ or "appropriating" to myself the grace of God. If that were the case, I would certainly not be receiving the kingdom of God as a little child.

Nay, to believe is not only to see that I am as helpless as a little child, but to acknowledge it as well. *Then,* and not before, have I become as a little child, one which puts forth no opposition to the salvation which *God* accomplishes.

As long as I, according to my inherent nature, think that I must have a part and that I must *assist* the Saviour in accomplishing my salvation, whether it be by repentance, contrition, or faith, so long do I put forth opposition to the salvation of God, whether I myself realize it or not.

During this time, therefore, the aim of God's quiet but purposive work is to *kill* me, that is, get me to lay down all opposition, which in turn means to get me to acknowledge that I can do absolutely nothing but get in the way of God.

From the moment I *acknowledge* this, God is free to impart unto me His whole salvation, as unto a little child.

This Biblical view of faith has now afforded us an insight into the remarkable, in fact, almost self-contradictory, condition of this seeking soul: He believes in the grace of God, but he does not dare to regard himself as a recipient of divine grace, and that because of the protest of his new-born conscience.

Behold the wonderful miracle of God!

He has here brought forth faith, but in such a masterly

way that it has become the death of the old nature and not its salvation.

*

This condition of the seeking soul, which we by a paradoxical expression might call "the despair of faith," is, then, not a deficiency but a necessary process through which we must pass in order to attain that mature and fully developed faith which we call the *assurance of faith.*

Let us now look for a moment at the relationship between conscience and assurance.

Many think that we cannot speak of assurance in an awakened and repentant sinner until he has attained complete spiritual emancipation and has found rest in the finished work of Christ alone.

But this is not in harmony with the realities of life.

As we all know, some awakened souls attain inner joy and peace very quickly, even though, as noted above, they often lose it after awhile and must pass through the same struggles as other awakened souls.

Likewise, we all know also that those awakened souls which are projected immediately into an inward struggle and into distress of conscience by no means walk in constant darkness. Not at all; now and then they, too, experience assurance and joy. As a rule this does not last very long at a time, and usually, too, things become just that much darker afterwards.

What was it that afforded them these more or less brief seasons of assurance?

It seems to me that we find the clearest answer in the apostle's words about assurance in I John 3:19: "Hereby shall we know that we are of the truth, and shall assure our heart before him."

As indicated previously, the expression "heart" here most certainly means conscience. This tells us therefore that assurance is contingent upon our conscience being assured before God.

When does our conscience become thus assured?

When conscience can say what it wishes without being hindered. And when it can get us to heed and to submit to its behests.

That is precisely how it happens that a seeking soul receives assurance during the brief seasons we have noted. Conscience is permitted to declare itself about sin as before. But at the same time the seeking sinner experiences in his soul during these brief seasons *grace which he can feel,* and which makes him think that he appears in a different light before God. He experiences fellowship with God, a fellowship which is rich and strong and which is unmediated by him. Now he loves God, yea, inexpressibly. Now he delights in prayer and in meditation upon the Word. Now he loves the children of God; now he hates sin in all its forms. Now he works and sacrifices willingly and gladly for the sake of the kingdom of God.

His conscience is at such a time, therefore, assured before God. It does not protest against believing the forgiveness of sins. It permits the sinner to *appropriate unto himself* all the things which he also formerly believed in, but which he hesitated to make his own.

But this assurance lasts only as long as the sinner *feels* the grace of God.

When this felt grace disappears, either suddenly or by gradually ebbing away, then his conscience again protests against believing the forgiveness of sins. And as a rule the seeker after God thereupon accuses himself of having been beguiled by his imagination, or of having practised self-deception, or of having entertained spiritual pride in believing that he was a child of God.

What is fundamentally wrong with assurance of this kind? The *foundation* is too weak.

Some go still further and say that the foundation is entirely false. They say that the seeking soul is here relying upon himself and not upon Christ. Therefore the assurance which he had could not and should not endure.

I cannot, however, pass such judgment upon this type of assurance.

This seeker is not relying upon himself. On the contrary, he is exceedingly circumspect, and afraid of himself and everything that he himself does. He has in fact become imbued with a holy mistrust of himself.

Nay, it is Christ in whom he places his confidence.

True enough, not in Christ *for us,* but in Christ *in us.* It is what *Christ* has done in him that makes him peaceful and glad. He experiences this as a *divine* operation within himself, not as something that he himself has produced. It is this that gives him this entirely new peace and rest.

This is also why his assurance is so brief, and why it fails him just when he needs it most, namely, when the felt grace of God disappears from his heart.

When he no longer feels a fervent love toward God and a burning hatred of sin, when his heart again becomes devoid of emotion, and when a feeling of indifference settles down upon him, then the *foundation of his forgiveness* disappears entirely.

*

Assurance becomes an entirely different matter when its foundation is Christ for us. Not until then do we gain full assurance, that is, complete and fully mature assurance. The aforementioned assurance is an incomplete one, an immature form of the assurance of faith.

The full assurance of faith, too, is dependent upon

conscience being assured before God, upon conscience being permitted to assert itself and be heeded in all things.

But here a new element enters into the situation.

That which now assures the conscience before God is still the work of Christ, not the work of Christ in us, however, but the work of Christ for us.

By a divine miracle, which is just as mysterious as the rest of God's miracles, the seeking soul through his new-born conscience begins to "hear" the word of the cross, hear it in such a way that he feels that it is *God* that is speaking to him. He hears the *full* Gospel of the cross, that which God would have him, a lost soul, hear about salvation. He now "sees" the Lamb of God who bore the sins of the world. God has now "revealed His Son" to him.

His conscience has truly become assured before God.

Now it can say anything that it desires both about sin and about grace. Now it can deliver its whole *accusation,* but also proclaim complete *absolution.* It is therefore *assured before God.*

It follows, then, that I possess this assurance only as long as I see these two things *simultaneously*: all of my sinfulness and all of God's grace.

A question: The awakened and repentant soul, who by the law of God and his new-born conscience has been crushed and condemned to death, why does he not experience *at once* the miracle just mentioned, by which he would be enabled to "hear" the word of the cross in such a way that he would be completely set free and would attain assurance?

This question is a source of annoyance to many, not only *before* they have the experience of being set free, but also after. It is, moreover, a deep and difficult question. And I do not know whether we shall ever find a *complete* answer to it.

But we can at least find a partial answer, and that in connection with that deep and mysterious aspect of faith which we have previously discussed. Faith is the work of God, the gift of God. This must be clearly impressed upon us, otherwise we will be "stealing" it from God. And if we could completely "solve" the question of faith, then faith would not be what it is. Nor would we be what we are, sinners lost and condemned in ourselves.

*

After the inquiry we have now made into the killing work of conscience, some might perhaps think that an awakened soul does not attain to faith at all until he has received assurance, or at least has had his old nature put to death by the law.

There have been and still are many who think this.

They think that as long as the awakened soul still struggles with the law, he cannot as yet be under grace. As yet nothing new has been born within him; he is still struggling along with his old nature's view of both God and of himself. He is striving, moreover, in the strength of his old nature.

Not until he receives the full light of God concerning his sinfulness and his lost condition, and not until he receives the full light concerning God's finished salvation in Christ, does he experience the double miracle which makes him a Christian, namely, justification and regeneration.

This view seems logically correct and incontrovertible.

But it is consistent neither with the Scriptures nor with experience.

I shall not here go into the relationship between faith and assurance, but refer those who would like to know more about this to the chapter entitled "Faith and Assurance" in my book *Under His Wings*.

At this point I should like to call attention briefly to the disciples as they were *before the death of Jesus*.

They are described as believers, as we all know. Jesus says that they were clean because of the word which He had spoken to them and which they had believed (John 15:3). They were, therefore, justified, that is, free from the guilt of sin.

But of how much of their sinfulness had they become aware up to this time?

And how much of Christ's vicarious suffering and death had they made their own up to this time?

The Gospels do not leave us in doubt concerning this. They relate with amazing candor that the disciples did not even understand that Jesus must suffer and die for their sins. See Luke 18:34, and especially Peter's rebuke of Jesus when the latter began to speak of His suffering and death (Matthew 16:22-23). This passage makes it clear that they did not even understand *why* Jesus had to suffer and die. The mystery of the cross was still completely veiled to them. But from this it is also clear that they were not fully aware of their own sinfulness and lost condition.

Still the Scriptures say that they were believers and that they were justified.

How are we to understand this?

Just as it is written. When they met Jesus and heard Him speak, they began to realize their sinfulness to such an extent and to such depths that they turned to Jesus and confessed to Him everything of which they were accused by their consciences.

And Jesus deemed this acknowledgment and this confession sufficient.

Their faith in Jesus was equally immature and imperfect. They had no conception, for instance, of even the fundamental thing in connection with the redemptive work of Christ.

Wherein, then, did their faith consist?

They had allowed themselves to be judged by the preaching of Jesus concerning sin. And their conscience had driven them to Christ. True, they did not realize to any great extent what they had in Him. But they did confess those sins of which they had been made aware, and they did look to Him for their whole salvation. As revelation progressed and their consciences became more sensitive, they began to see more and more both their own sinfulness and what they possessed in their Saviour.

This is precisely what takes place in the awakened soul of today.

He has *faith* from the moment that he honestly submits to the behests of his awakened and new-born conscience and goes to Christ with the sin and distress of which he has been made aware.

To begin with he most likely does not see any more of his sinfulness than did the disciples before the death of Jesus. But he is a *believer,* nevertheless, as they were, provided he does not dissimulate, provided he does not conceal or cloak any sin of which his conscience accuses him.

Faith is here, as always, the looking unto Jesus which is born out of distress of conscience. And that regardless of how much or how little conscience as yet has been awakened, only provided it is permitted to drive us to Christ, to Christ, be it observed, to be *saved from that of which we have been made aware by our conscience.*

To begin with, the awakened soul has very little insight into the mystery of the Gospel also. He does not by any means realize to the full what the cross of Christ really means to him.

The same was true of the disciples before the death of Jesus.

But he clings to Jesus and His full salvation, even though he as yet understands but very little of all that the Saviour means to him.

And this was the situation also in which the disciples were before the death of Jesus.

Conscience and the New Man

"I thank God, whom I serve from my forefathers in a pure conscience." —II TIMOTHY 1:3.

CONSCIENCE says: Thou shalt! Thou shalt not! Can this be consistent with the new heart which the believer has received, with his spirit of free will?

Many think that the believer should have nothing more to do with such things as the demands of conscience and the requirements of the law.

They say:

"Christ is the end of the law" (Romans 10:4).

"Having abolished in his flesh the enmity, even the law of commandments contained in ordinances" (Ephesians 2:15).

"The law was given through Moses; grace and truth came through Jesus Christ" (John 1:17).

"Ye are not under the law, but under grace" (Romans 6:14).

"Ye also were made dead through the law through the body of Christ" (Romans 7:4).

The law belonged to the Old Covenant. The New Testament believer is free from the law. To speak of the duties of a believer is therefore to put him in bondage under the law again. This constitutes unevangelical preaching. The believer has had the law written in his heart; the love of God has now been shed abroad in his heart by the Holy Spirit. Therefore he does the will of God in willing love and obedience.

It is not necessary, therefore, for the believer to hear

the requirements of the law proclaimed. To him one should preach only the grace of God in Christ Jesus. It is grace which is the motivating power in his new life. And even though he should become slothful in his Christian life, still the law must not be preached to him; for the law can never bring forth or increase the love of God within his heart. Not at all; preach grace only also to careless Christians. That will melt away their love of self and their opposition to the Spirit of God, and so rekindle their love to God that they will freely and obediently do His will again.

Here truth and falsehood are mingled together in a most bewildering fashion.

The element of truth in this viewpoint is that the law has been abolished *as a way of salvation*.

The Jews misunderstood the law which God had revealed to them and thought that they by fulfilling the law could win God's favor and gain His forgiveness. It is this especially that the Apostle Paul contends against, showing that fallen man cannot fulfil the law of God and thus win the favor of God.

Wherefore God ordained salvation to be by *faith*.

"For what the law could not do, in that it was weak through the flesh, God, sending his own Son in the likeness of sinful flesh, condemned sin in the flesh" (Romans 8:3). "But now apart from the law a righteousness of God hath been manifested . . . through faith in Jesus Christ" (Romans 3:21-22). "But to him that worketh not, but believeth on him that justifieth the ungodly, his faith is reckoned for righteousness" (Romans 4:5).

The error in connection with the above mentioned view arises when people think that the law has been abrogated in *all* respects. The law cannot thus be abrogated or abolished. For the law is nothing less than an expression of the will of God. And the will of God is, as we know, as eternal and unchangeable as God Himself.

It is true that the Scriptures say that the Mosaic ordinances have been abolished (Hebrews 9:9-10). They were done away with because they were only a preparatory and imperfect expression of the will of God; they were only "carnal ordinances imposed until a time of reformation."

Jesus therefore also said that He did not come to destroy the law. On the contrary, He came to fulfill the revelation of divine law which was as yet incomplete, as we have indicated above (Matthew 5:17). Thus we see that in the Sermon on the Mount He sharpens the ancient requirements of the law, showing us what God's will really was with respect to the outward commandments of the Old Testament.

*

But though this is clear to us, still the question we have propounded remains as much unanswered as ever: How can the categorical, thou shalt! thou shalt not! be made to harmonize with the new heart and the willing spirit of the believer?

If the law is written in the heart, as the Scriptures say in Jeremiah 31:33-34, is any other commandment necessary?

Are not duty and love irreconcilable opposites?

Does not duty go out when love enters? And does not love pass away when our whole relationship to God becomes one of duty?

Here again we come in contact with one of the deepest mysteries of life.

The mysterious thing about life is, as we know, that it oftentimes contains elements which according to our ideas seem to contradict one another. So also here.

Let us begin with the writing of the law in the heart.

That is, of course, what takes place in the new birth. At that time we receive a new attitude of heart, one of love toward God. But love toward God is, obviously, love toward the will of God. This is emphasized, if possible even more strongly, when it is said that we have received the seed of God, have become partakers of the divine nature (I John 3:9; II Peter 1:4).

But even if we, as a result of the new birth, *love* the will of God, still we must *know* it.

And it is through the Word that God has revealed His will. The believer, therefore, has not by the new birth and his new attitude of heart become independent of the outward Word; on the contrary, he has become bound to it in a new way. He knows it now as the Word of *God* and therefore, too, loves it.

Meanwhile God does *not only* use the outward Word to make known to us His will. As we have shown above, *conscience* is the means by which God brings the outward Word into our inner being. Consequently the believer will be independent of conscience as little as he will of the Word. The two belong inseparably together, as God Himself has ordained it.

We can now answer the question propounded above with regard to the relationship between conscience and the believer's new attitude of heart. And the answer is this:

The new birth does not put the believer into a relationship of opposition to his conscience, but, on the contrary, puts the believer into *the normal relationship* with his conscience. In fact, this very thing is without doubt the greatest miracle of all in connection with the new birth.

Our old nature's relation to conscience is abnormal and sinful. Sin never stands forth as clearly at any time as it does in our relation to conscience. Our old nature feels that conscience is a burden. It feels that the categorical, absolute, and inappealable judgments of conscience are unpleasant interruptions in its self-seeking and ease-loving existence.

This is the nature of our inherent and deep-seated wickedness.

We do not only commit sin; we feel unpleasantly affected when we are disturbed in our sins by a conscience which will not yield to evil. Nor is that all. We even try to silence our conscience in order to be able to continue in sin undisturbed.

Now look at the new relationship to conscience which has come into being as a result of the new birth.

The new man within us loves God, and therefore loves everything that is from God; also conscience, which in a wonderful way brings the voice of God into the very soul of man.

For that reason an awakened soul does not feel that his conscience is something foreign and inimical to him, but something that he knows and loves. It is like a friend who brings him a message from God Himself, one who helps him diligently and without dissimulation both to *know* and to *do* the will of God. He rejoices, therefore, the more strongly and clearly it speaks to him.

It is no doubt this relationship that James has in mind when he speaks of "the law of liberty," and describes it as perfect (James 1:25; 2:12). Here he combines liberty with law. They seem mutually to exclude each other. But life unites them—at least regenerate life. For love is the union of liberty and law. It is law-bound liberty and voluntary allegiance to law.

God Himself lives His perfect life from eternity and to eternity according to this law of liberty. He is *bound* by the law of love to such an extent that He cannot act contrary to love. But His being bound is voluntary. Herein consists the very liberty of God. He never wills anything but that which is consistent with the law of love.

By the new birth He has in a creative way put fallen man into the same voluntary relationship to the law. Of course, only by way of a beginning; for even a regenerate man can carry it out only very imperfectly in his life. But a beginning nevertheless has been made. And He who has begun the good work will Himself perfect it until the day of Jesus Christ.

*

Let us now look a little more in detail into the significance of conscience in the life of a regenerate individual.

What is its significance in connection with sanctification?

In answering this question most people would no doubt say: Its purpose is to keep alive our sense of sin. And this is right and in accordance with the Scriptures. "Through the law cometh the knowledge of sin" (Romans 3:20). This knowledge comes, not only during the period of awakening and conversion, but throughout all of life. Only in this way can that hunger and thirst be created which can be satisfied at no other place but at the cross of Christ. And thus the law continues to be our tutor to bring us to Christ (Galatians 3:24).

But at the same time our conscience is intended to preserve us from self-deception.

By its unimpeachable honesty and its aggressive power it warns us against that spirit of guile which is our greatest foe, from the very beginning of our awakening to our dying hour. The Scriptures say something about the heart of man being more deceitful than all else. But the most tragic of all is that man desires to be deceived. This is the natural man's greatest misfortune and his greatest danger.

This danger pursues us also after we have experienced the new birth, for we have our old nature with us at all times. And with it we have that spiritual dead-weight which inexorably draws us down into self-deception, unless God through our conscience succeeds in persuading us to give heed to this danger every day of our lives.

It is *dead faith* which is the real danger in connection with self-deception.

What is dead faith?

Pontoppidan answers this with masterly clearness: "Dead faith is a false idea which men entertain about receiving grace although they will not repent."

The believer has through the enlightenment of the Gospel gained an insight into that mystery of grace that God loves us for Christ's sake even before we have made any attempt to keep His law. But this knowledge entails a great risk, as is true of all of God's gifts. God has given us this knowledge for our blessing, but it may become even as great a curse to us.

Our old nature would undoubtedly like to make use of this clear insight into the mystery of grace for its own purposes. And the result would be a comfortable, easy type of Christianity, involving no serious struggle against sinful habits, no honest and unequivocal reconciliations with God, and no sacrifice or self-denial. Instead we would have a continuous taking refuge in theoretical knowledge about the grace of God.

Thus to misuse the grace of God is what the older generation referred to by the expression, "to sin against grace."

The expression is an unfortunate and misleading one, for no one can sin against grace. Grace always looses us inwardly from sin, that is, if we truly experience the grace of God. What they really meant was that we can make use of our theoretical knowledge of grace in such a way as to excuse our sins and exempt ourselves from the daily accounting before God and the daily struggle against sin.

This will occur without fail in the life of every Christian unless his new born conscience daily exposes and punishes this deception.

*

As our conscience becomes enlightened through diligent use of the Bible, it will bring the whole outward as well as the inner life of the believer into the light of the Word of God, and point out even the minutest infractions of God's holy and loving will, in deed, word, thought, imagination, and desire. And not least our sins of *omission,* because they so clearly indicate our lack of love both to God and man.

Here let us note further that conscience places before us at this time a goal which is nothing short of *perfection,* according to Jesus' own words, "Ye therefore shall be perfect, as your heavenly Father is perfect" (Matthew 5:48). Our conscience always judges our lives in the light of that which is perfect, resulting in conscience finding us guilty on *many* counts. We are in truth made to feel that "in many things we all stumble" (James 3:2).

Conscience not only convicts us daily, continuously, of our many mistakes and our sins of omission, but that which is more serious, it unceasingly convicts us of the fact that our *attitude of heart* is wholly in conflict with the will of God. Many of our words and deeds appear to be outwardly good, so that our fellow men may perhaps even value both them and us highly, but our conscience says:

Your motives are not good. It was not in love that you did this or said that!

Here, too, conscience compares us with that which is *perfect*.

This crushes us completely. For in the light of perfection nothing in us is whole or pure. Everything is tainted by selfish by-motives, which enter by stealth even into our best deeds. We experience how egoism taints even our most self-sacrificing services both to God and man.

Our predicament becomes most unfortunate of all when conscience focuses our attention upon *our relationship to God*.

We no doubt speak the truth when we say that we cannot live without God. But is it because we love Him? Is it for the sake of God alone that we keep near to Him? Is it not much more for *our own* sake? Is it not myself I think of most in all my associations with God?

Is it not all a question of doing my duty, nothing more?

My soul is withered, empty, and callous. Where is the life that is hid in God with Christ Jesus?

As a matter of fact, my heart is not merely empty as far as the fear of God is concerned, it is full of other interests, which in and by themselves are perhaps not sinful, but which nevertheless are harmful, because they crowd out the one thing needful.

Nor is that all. My heart is filled with many desires, thoughts, and imaginations which are downright sinful.

Then comes the question: Am I really a child of God?

If I were a child of God, certainly my life and my whole attitude of heart would be different from what they are.

"To me it seems I fall far short
Of what my heart would have me be,"

sings Per Nordsletten, a refrain which occurs again and
again in the perplexed and weary heart of a child of
God.

*

See what God achieves in the daily life of the believer
through conscience!

This is the *daily* putting to death which God works
within us in order to preserve us from laying the foundation of our salvation in ourselves.

Thus He drives us each day to Christ and His cross.

Thus He makes us hunger and thirst in such a way that
it is impossible for us to live even a single day without
the living waters and the bread which cometh down from
heaven that men might live.

Thus He crushes our hearts each day, hearts which
otherwise would stiffen into routine godliness and into
faith in its own Christianity instead of in its Saviour.

Thus He keeps us among the poor in spirit, who always
need grace. Who not only know about grace, think about
grace, and speak about grace, but who live by grace.

Here we touch upon the great mystery in connection
with a life of faith. Here we gain an insight into the
fact that a life of faith is also replete with suspense. We
see that conscience creates an element of suspense which
involves our faith in a *constant struggle*.

Luther says somewhere that faith can survive only as
long as it struggles. He had in mind the struggle of
which we are speaking here, the struggle of faith to hold
fast to grace and to sonship with God also when our
heart condemns us because of our failings in daily life.

This suspense is a part of living faith and cannot be dissociated from it. If it is removed from the life of faith, we will have a dead faith, a faith which holds fast to the free grace of God with the intellect but which does not give conscience an opportunity to condemn sin and give the sinner that strong feeling of unworthiness which he cannot resist feeling when he is made by his conscience to stand before the living God.

This suspense cannot be eliminated by *theoretical* insight into the mystery of the Gospel. Not even a rich and prolonged experience with the free grace of God can remove this suspense.

However, life never follows straight lines.

We find in our experience that this suspense is not equally strong at all times in our life. That is because life moves in waves.

At the same time let us note that it is not necessarily the poorest type of Christians that has difficulties such as these in believing the grace of God and holding fast to sonship with Him. On the contrary, we note that the most spiritual, warm-hearted, and self-sacrificing types of Christians are frequently subject to strong attacks of doubt and difficulty in connection with faith. Thus Luther, the great hero of faith, often had great difficulty in believing even the daily forgiveness of sins.

As I see it, this suspense continues to increase rather than decrease.

This, too, is due to our conscience. The more sensitive and discriminating our conscience becomes, the *more* it will accuse us, the more deeply it will affect us.

A rich and long experience with the grace of God will only serve to intensify the conflict. With redoubled weight and seriousness the question will arise: Can you be a child of God, in view of the fact that God's abundant grace has been so fruitless and vain in your heart and in your life? Is not this proof that your faith is dead, and that you are misusing the grace of God?

Here also a living faith will emerge victorious and once again find *rest* in the grace of God. But only after a struggle. Here too it is conscience which *drives* our faith, drives it to Christ. For faith is, as previously noted, that looking unto Christ which is born out of the distress of conscience.

Distress of conscience is therefore not only the mother of faith; it also renews our faith, and keeps it continually alive. It is that which preserves our faith as a *living* faith.

This complicated faith, composed as it is of several elements, has been given unique expression in the remarkable words of the apostle: "as sorrowful, yet always rejoicing" (II Corinthians 6:10).

*

This brings us to *the deep groaning* in the soul of the believer.

A Christian experiences a painful restlessness, which never completely subsides, a chronic pain, which increases rather than diminishes in intensity.

This restlessness, as previously stated, may very easily bewilder the believer.

He begins to fear that there is something in his relationship to God which is not as it should be. However, this deep groaning is not a symptom of illness affecting his life of faith. It is, on the contrary, a sign of health.

It shows, in the first place, that his *love* toward God is sound and pure, that he experiences pain when he grieves the Saviour, who has suffered so bitterly for all his unfaithfulness and disobedience.

This groaning shows, in the second place, that his conscience is tender, being grieved by even the smallest sin.

This deep groaning within the soul of the believer is there for a twofold purpose.

In the first place, it should cause us inwardly to have nothing to do with sin. The aim of sanctification is, as we know, to cause us to break with sin within. We know also that it is by His love alone that God can loose our hearts from sin. It is also clear to us now that it is through an awakened conscience that God can reach us with His love, reach us in such a way that we feel that it becomes more and more unendurable to sin against such a love.

This deep groaning is therefore the surest sign that God's love is being permitted to do its saving work within our soul. And the deeper this pain becomes, the more *spiritual* our abstaining from sin becomes.

Our striving against sin arises from various motives, concerning which we oftentimes are not clear in our own minds.

At times we struggle against sin because we fear its unfortunate consequences both for time and for eternity. At other times our struggle against sin is prompted by our own wise calculations; we conclude that we would profit most by not yielding to it.

But this comes very close to casting out the devil by Beelzebub.

We achieve real victory over sin only when we can say with Joseph: "How can I do this great wickedness and sin against God?" Not until then do we really abstain from sin as sin, as that which is contrary to the will of God.

In the second place, this deep groaning has for its purpose to help us to lift up our eyes and look forward to the day of redemption. This sigh is a mighty lever, which quietly but assuredly leads our earth-bound nature to look upward towards our heavenly fatherland.

In other words its purpose is to impart to us a true *yearning for our home in heaven.*

No doubt there is a good deal of yearning for heaven which is not esteemed very highly by those in the beyond. Our earthly plans are crossed; adversity and tribulation set in; everything goes wrong. Then we begin to yearn for heaven.

Such longing for the heavenly homeland is nothing but veiled egoism and fear of suffering.

True longing for heaven, on the other hand, springs from deep sorrow for having sinned against God, and is a longing for the day when we no more shall defile our souls by a single sin, no longer offend any of our fellow men by our self-love, no longer grieve our Saviour by disobedience or unfaithfulness of any kind.

*

So far we have spoken chiefly about the *negative* significance of conscience in relation to the sanctification of the believer.

As I see it, that is the only side that is touched upon in our day when men speak of the relationship between the law and conscience. The Scriptures, however, speak without a doubt also about the *positive* significance of conscience in connection with sanctification.

"For what the law could not do, in that it was weak through the flesh, God, sending his own Son in the likeness of sinful flesh and for sin, condemned sin in the flesh: that the ordinances of the law might be fulfilled in us, who walk not after the flesh, but after the Spirit" (Romans 8:3-4).

Most people with whom I have spoken regarding this passage read it wrong. They read it as though it said: that the law might be fulfilled in Christ. And this is what is ordinarily preached, so far as I have been able to observe.

But the Scriptures speak otherwise. We read: "that the ordinance of the law might be fulfilled *in us.*"

Here the apostle tells us briefly and clearly what the purpose of God's salvation is. It is that the ordinances of the law might be fulfilled, not only in Christ, but in us also.

In like manner the apostle says that God could not secure the fulfilment of these requirements through the law. It was impossible through the law, he says. The law was powerless through the flesh, which is enmity against God, and therefore also against the will of God, the divine law.

It became evident that God did not secure the fulfilment of even the *outward* requirements of the law in Old Testament times. And it became even more impossible to secure the fulfilment of the law's requirements after Christ had shown that these requirements are directed first and foremost towards our *attitude of heart,* and that with respect to this attitude the law contains essentially only one requirement, and that is, to *love.*

Because it was impossible for the law to change either the life or the attitude of heart of sinful man, God sent His Son to save man. And now the apostle says further that God's purpose in sending the Son was that the law might be fulfilled *in us.*

His incarnation, atonement, resurrection, and ascension, and the outpouring of the Holy Spirit all have therefore this one objective. Likewise everything that He works within us: awakening, repentance, faith, justifi-

cation, regeneration, and sanctification. All these divine
acts of mercy have as their objective the fulfilling of the
law of God, declares the apostle.

Let us then take a brief retrospect and see how God
accomplishes this.

After God by the atonement has made it possible to
receive the sinner into fellowship with Himself, He sets
in motion the process of *awakening*. It consists, as we
have observed above, in a new-creation of the conscience,
as a result of which the sinner not only acquires *knowledge* concerning the requirements of the law, but experiences them as the requirements of *God,* requirements,
be it noted well, that he feels himself absolutely compelled to fulfil.

In *repentance* the sinner decides to submit to the authoritative demands of his conscience, to fulfil the requirements of the law, and thus make his life conform to the
will of God.

By the choice which he thus makes in repentance he
attains simultaneously to *faith*.

He believes in the law of God, believes that God has
the right to demand of him that which is absolute and
perfect, and proceeds therefore forthwith to fulfil the
demands of the law. Moreover, he continues to do this,
even though he experiences daily the impossibility of its
achievement.

Meanwhile he has *misunderstood* the fulfilling of the
law.

He has misunderstood its *purpose*. He thinks that fulfilling the law will bring him salvation. At first he misunderstands this in a gross way, and thinks that by doing
the will of God he can move God to assume a friendly
attitude towards him and that he can thus win the favor
of God.

Afterwards he sees that this is impossible.

But his misunderstanding of the fulfilment of the law persists, in a finer form however. He thinks now that he must fulfil the law before God can impart to him His divine grace and make him a partaker of the finished redemption of Christ Jesus.

This misunderstanding is *unavoidable* to the natural man in the early stages of his conversion. Moreover, it is this which creates that hopeless struggle which the Scriptures speak of as the *killing* of the old ego.

Through this being put to death the seeking soul in turn acquires the inner ear which enables him to "hear" the Gospel, the inner eye which enables him to "behold" the Lamb of God.

He now discovers his mistake. The mystery of the Gospel is unveiled to him: God *justifies* the ungodly. He sees now that God loves and forgives him for Christ's sake, even before he is able to fulfil a single one of the law's requirements.

He discovers now that he has turned the thing upside down. The situation is not such that he must fulfil the law in order to move God to love and forgive him, but vice versa: God loves and forgives him for Christ's sake in order that by so doing He might enable him to fulfil the requirements of the law.

In the *new birth* he receives that attitude of heart which is the indispensable requirement for fulfilling the law. In it there is imparted to him that *love* which wills what God wills.

*

Behold, God has now achieved His purpose with His salvation: that the ordinances of the law might be fulfilled in us.

Not perfectly, it is true, only in part, and very defectively. But a beginning has nevertheless been made.

And a right beginning it is.

For God has begun in the heart, begun by creating a new inner man.

Sanctification consists now in this one thing, and this only, to be certain that this attitude of heart penetrates through and becomes the determining factor in our whole being, in our spirit, soul, and body (I Thessalonians 5:23).

This God accomplishes by the aid of our *conscience*.

After it has become enlightened by the Word of God with regard to all the things pertaining to the will of God, it does nothing else day after day and all day long but to point out the requirements of the law to the believer. Not in vague generalities, but in a practical and concrete way, showing us very definitely how we should go about loving God and our neighbor.

As stated above, conscience always holds before us the ideal of *perfection*—nothing less than that which is perfect.

Sanctification is nothing less than *God* daily exercising us imperfect but regenerate human beings in living *the perfect life.*

This is what creates the element of *suspense* in sanctification.

This is also the *faith* element in sanctification. On our part sanctification is essentially a matter of faith. And faith in this instance consists of this one thing, that without compromise or concessions of any kind we hold fast the requirements of the law: that we, imperfect as we are, must do the things that are perfect. As Jesus has put it briefly and simply: "Ye therefore shall be perfect, as your heavenly Father is perfect" (Matthew 5:48).

But this is also the *dangerous* aspect of sanctification, in two respects.

It is easy for us, in the first place, to forget the mystery of the Gospel in the midst of the struggle known as sanctification, and to slip back into bondage under the law. And think that it is the fulfilling of the law on our part which causes God to love us.

And that God does not love us when we make very slow progress or when we fail entirely to fulfil the law.

The second danger is much worse and more common.

When day after day we see that it is not possible for imperfect mortals such as we are to practice perfection, then we are tempted to lessen the requirements of the law. The impossible is impossible, we say. Not even God can expect the impossible.

Consequently we tone down the requirements to what an ordinary imperfect mortal can just about manage to keep. Which will as a rule mean that we will conduct ourselves about as other Christians with whom we are acquainted, or at best as the most outstanding Christians within the circle of our acquaintanceship.

By so doing we have, in the first place, removed the element of suspense from sanctification.

At the same time we have removed the element of faith.

We have followed reason, which says, of course, that it is impossible for imperfect men to practice perfection. The result is that we have brought down the requirements of God to *human* levels.

Faith, on the other hand, believes in the requirements of God, even though they are impossible. And does not give up the requirement of perfection, even though it sees its own imperfect fulfilment of the law each day.

Are we not here dealing with one of the chief dangers in connection with the Christian life of our day?

The fact that we make so little progress in sanctification, that there is so much wan and withered Christianity amongst us, and that notwithstanding our clear and evangelical Gospel light, is it not due to the fact that the very possibility of growth in our Christian life has been cut off at this point?

We preachers are most to blame here.

Many of us have forgotten the law, and preach only the Gospel.

Some of us, it is true, preach the law, the whole unmitigated law, but only to teach that through the law comes the knowledge of sin and that the law is our tutor to bring us to Christ.

But as soon as we have brought the sinner to Christ our preaching of the law ceases. We do not think that he is supposed to hear any more about the requirements of the law. That is, he is not supposed to hear about them as requirements for him to fulfil in his own life. He is only supposed to hear the law from now on for the purpose of being tutored unto Christ.

We forget God's purpose in saving sinners: that the ordinances of the law might be fulfilled *in us*.

What can the reason be that we overlook this clear Scriptural truth?

We do not succeed, as did Jesus and the apostles, in combining a proper presentation of the law with the preaching of the Gospel. We are of the opinion that to preach the requirements of the law to believers would be to lead them into bondage under the law again and obscure the light of the Gospel to them.

We do not see that the believer, for the very reason that he believes the Gospel and lives by grace, not only should but desires to live according to the law of God, as the apostle says: "Do we then make the law of none effect through faith? God forbid: nay, we establish the law" (Romans 3:31).

Therefore not only *should* the law be preached to the believer—he himself *desires* it.

But the preaching of the law to the believer must be *evangelical,* that is, we must preach that the law must be fulfilled by us, not in order that we may be loved by God, but because we are loved by Him, in Christ, our Substitute.

The Degeneration and Death of Conscience

THE life which our conscience lives is, as all life, subject to the law of growth, development, and fruition.

This development and fruition may be either toward the good or toward the bad.

First let us follow the development in the direction of evil, the *degeneration* of conscience, its deterioration.

As we have seen in the preceding, conscience functions wholly instinctively and intuitively. That is, it is not set in motion by our will or by any conscious effort on our part. On the contrary, it frequently raises its voice in *opposition* both to our will and to our thoughts.

But this does not mean that our conscience lives and develops independently of our consciousness and our will. No normal person can avoid having conscience *begin* its authoritative work within his soul. But in what way this activity is to *continue* depends upon his will.

Which means more specifically that he can and should by his will determine whether his conscience is to be permitted to do its work in peace and thus through growth and fruition reach the goal of its development, or whether it is to be hindered, weakened, and finally completely destroyed. For there is an intimate, organic connection between conscience and will.

Whenever conscience speaks, its message is directed to our will. That is why Immanuel *Kant* spoke of the *categorical imperative*, the categorical demands which conscience directs to our will.

The attitude which our will assumes towards this categorical imperative is the determining factor in connection with the future development and work of our conscience.

If the will accedes to the demands of conscience, our conscience will grow and develop. No other means are necessary for strengthening conscience. It is as with our lungs. They grow and develop by breathing, by inhaling and exhaling air.

But if our will does not submit to the judgment of our conscience, our conscience will be weakened. The disobedience of our will reacts upon our conscience in such a way that it gradually loses its ability to issue categorical demands.

To begin with it is very painful not to give heed to the authoritative voice of our conscience and to act in direct contravention of its demands. During this time, therefore, no one can endure to do so very long at a time. Accordingly, we vacillate between obedience and disobedience, and feel inwardly quieted every time we heed our conscience.

But as the wicked will develops and establishes itself, it becomes more and more difficult to submit to the warnings of conscience. As a result we have a bad conscience, which fills the soul with unrest and anxiety, and darkens everything, even the brightest and best things in life. This no man can endure.

A person who persists in his disobedience and refuses to heed his conscience will instinctively seek to *deaden* his conscience, silence it, in order not to be continually distressed and annoyed by it, by its warnings before a deed is committed or by its annoying restlessness afterwards.

There are many ways of deadening one's conscience.

May I here mention the following:

Some abandon themselves to drinking and carousing.

Intoxicating liquor vitiates the higher capacities of the soul to such an extent that contact with the higher functions of the soul is thereby lost. Hence conscience can no longer gain access to the soul.

The more spineless persons, those who are unable to control themselves, usually abandon themselves to what might be termed a permanent state of intoxication, and sink down quickly into a life of lust and shame.

The stronger willed ones become moderate drinkers, seeking a milder form of exhilaration, not that of excessive intoxication. They frequently become addicts of morphine or cocaine.

Others try to deaden their consciences by concentrating on their *work* to such an extent that it exceeds all bounds. And it would seem that they succeed fairly well, especially if their work is interesting and fascinating. They give themselves no rest. In fact, they are afraid to rest, because then their serious thoughts return to them and they become aware again of their evil conscience. Consequently they work continually, until far into the night. Then they drop off to sleep—instantly. They fear nothing as much as lying awake at night.

Others deaden their consciences more *artfully*. These are no doubt the greater in number.

And this method of deadening the conscience is unquestionably the more dangerous and results in the greater damage.

There is what is known as *wish-thinking,* that is, thinking which does not follow the rules of logic, but the whims and notions of our wishes.

Then to strengthen or defend our wishes we try to justify them on logical grounds. It is not so much the truth; it is rather our own wishes that we seek to defend.

If our actions cannot be defended on *moral* grounds, we become the more zealous in our defense of them on *logical* grounds.

Thus that *deception* of character begins which consists in not only doing sin in the hour of trial, but afterwards lying to oneself in order to deaden one's evil conscience.

We lie ourselves away from our evil motive by saying that the reason why things went wrong when we were tempted was not that we *wanted* to sin; circumstances, other people, or our natural dispositions were to blame for the whole thing.

By so doing one lies oneself away from the deepest aspect of sin, namely, its guilt, the fact that I wanted to sin, that it was *my* act.

Here is the beginning of that *deceitful nature* which with devilish logic wards off every accusation of conscience.

This is what the apostle has in mind when he speaks of a branded conscience in I Timothy 4:2. It is as though he would say that the conscience is suffering from a wound made by branding, by searing or burning.

No doubt the apostle refers to the same thing when he speaks of a *defiled* conscience. Something unclean, something foreign, has penetrated into and is perverting the conscience.

We have already described how the *Jesuits* practice this perversion of conscience.

We find it in a little different form among the *Pharisees*. Their consciences were very scrupulous with regard to little things. Thus they were very strict regarding the giving of the tithe, giving a tenth part of even the smallest vegetables in their gardens. But the weighty matters of the law, justice, and mercy, and faith, they left undone

(Matthew 23:23). In fact they did not even blush to "devour widows' houses" (Matthew 23:14). They were so careful with regard to the ceremonial laws concerning cleansing that they would not enter into Pilate's hall during the trial of Jesus; otherwise they could not celebrate the Passover. But to condemn the Innocent One to death and even employ false witnesses to do so, that their consciences permitted them to do.

We speak of people *not having any conscience.* It is a strong expression, one which we no doubt are too hasty in using. Not to have a conscience means to be devoid of one entirely. Of course, we use the expression in a somewhat modified sense, meaning that a person is unfaithful to his conscience and heeds it only when it is convenient to do so, that is, when it is not unpleasant to do so or when one does not suffer any inconvenience by so doing.

For this reason we cannot rely upon such people.

When the Scriptures speak of people who *sleep,* it is the sleeping conscience that is meant. This sleep is a result of the deadening of which we have spoken in the preceding pages.

A sleeping conscience can be awakened. But experience teaches us that its sleep can be very deep indeed. A person can at times live horribly peacefully in his sins, and can often live that way a long time. Such people keep the functioning of their conscience in abeyance by force.

But notwithstanding all this such consciences can be awakened, at times even in persons of very advanced age. It depends upon the means they have used in deadening their consciences. If a person has employed deception, such as we have described above, an awakening becomes almost an impossibility, because deception leads to the *hardening* of the conscience.

This is spoken of in the Scriptures as the hardening of the heart (Ephesians 4:18). Or simply as a hardening (Romans 11:7; see also Hebrews 3:13, 15).

This condition represents the complete degeneration and definite death of conscience.

It is no longer possible to awaken such a conscience. Because of this condition such a person is eternally lost. For salvation cannot reach a person except through his conscience.

The Holy Spirit must convict man of sin, Jesus says (John 16:8). But when one's conscience has been burned out, a person can no longer be convicted. His conscience has lost the spiritual faculty of receiving and possessing a conviction.

This condition is spoken of in the Scriptures at times as *sin unto death* (I John 5:16) and at times as *blasphemy against the Spirit* (Matthew 12:31).

The Bible says expressly that there is no forgiveness for this sin.

It does not consist in any sinful act, no matter how gross it may be, but is a condition of the conscience, one which is the result of a shorter or longer development. More precisely defined, it is a fruit of the degeneration of conscience referred to above. It is therefore not purely and simply a result of opposition and disobedience to conscience, but of that inner deceit by which men lie themselves away from the *truth* spoken to them by their conscience.

The reason that this sin against conscience cannot be forgiven is not that it is so great that God will not forgive it. It is written: "God . . . would have all men to be saved, and come to the knowledge of the truth" (I Timothy 2:4).

Nor is it because this sin is so great that Jesus would

not or could not atone for it. It is written: "The blood of Jesus his Son cleanseth us from all sin" (I John 1:7).

By no means; this sin is unforgivable for the one and only reason that the man who has committed it has thrust his conscience from himself (I Timothy 1:19).

That organ in man which constitutes the point of contact for God's salvation has been wasted and destroyed. Man's last possibility of being saved has thus been lost, because sorrow for sin has become an impossibility.

This does not mean that all feeling of sin is gone.

On the contrary, Hebrews 10:27 says that the unforgivable sin will be accompanied by "a certain fearful expectation of judgment, and a fierceness of fire which shall devour the adversaries."

However, this is nothing but the "sorrow of the world" in its most aggravated form. By this is meant sorrow because of the consequences of sin, not because of sin itself, not because of the fact of having sinned against God.

If this sinner would repent and confess his sins, God would be ready to save him too. For it is written: "If we confess our sins, he is faithful to forgive us our sins, and to cleanse us from all unrighteousness" (I John 1:9).

Such a soul's eternal inability to be saved is due simply to the fact that he no longer has a conscience which can convict him of sin and make him willing to confess it before God.

When a man has reached this state, not even God has any other means of saving him.

Herein lies the terrible seriousness of it all.

God can create *a new man* within fallen man, but only in connection with the conscience of fallen man. God cannot create *a new conscience* in man after fallen man has deliberately and wilfully destroyed his powers of conscience.

Conscience is therefore *the irreplaceable thing* in human life.

It is that which makes us human beings.

The most fearful power therefore which man possesses is that he by his will can destroy the very humanity which is within himself, and thus make of himself, not an *animal,* but a *devil.*

The Growth and Fruition
of Conscience

*"But the end of the charge is love out of a pure
heart and a good conscience and faith unfeigned."*
—I Timothy 1:5.

AS we have observed above, conscience is not a
fully completed piece of psychological mecha-
nism. It is a living entity, subject to growth
and development.

This growth and development we have had to refer to
before in order to make clear what conscience is and how
it functions.

We saw at that time that the growth of conscience is
dependent upon a certain theoretical element, namely,
knowledge of the will of God.

The *form* of conscience is always the same, whether
one's knowledge of the will of God is great or small.
But the *content* of conscience is to the very highest degree dependent upon this knowledge.

If this knowledge is deficient, conscience will subjec-
tively authorize man to do things which are objectively
in conflict with the will of God. Thus a heathen is bound
by his conscience to kill his father's murderer.

Or, conversely, it will forbid acts which in themselves
are permissible, such, for instance, as eating horse flesh.

Here we might also mention "the weak," of whom Paul
speaks in I Corinthians, chapters 8 and 10. Their consciences forbade them to eat certain meat, which appar-
ently had been sold generally, but which was meat from
animals used in heathen sacrifices. These people felt that

by eating this meat they would be indirectly taking part in the worship of the heathen (I Corinthians 8:7; 10:25).

Here the apostle throws the light of the Gospel upon the situation by saying that there was no difference between this meat and other meat. "Nothing is unclean of itself" (Romans 14:14).

But, on the other hand, something was wrong also with the consciences of "the strong," the apostle says. They saw clearly that they, by virtue of their evangelical liberty, could eat this meat. In their opinion, moreover, it was their duty to make use of their Christian liberty and not let themselves be hindered by the unevangelical and legalistic viewpoint of the weak. "Why is my liberty judged by another conscience?" Thus the apostle cites their argument in I Corinthians 10:29.

The apostle now addresses these "strong" souls and says that their view regarding the meat was correct, but not their view of Christian liberty.

They *misused* their liberty when by eating this meat they laid a snare for "the weak," who thus yielded to the temptation to do the same, but with a bad conscience.

By so doing their conscience became *defiled* (I Corinthians 8:7). And if they had continued to do this they would have perished, the apostle continues in chapter 8, verse 11. For "whatsoever is not of faith is *sin*" (Romans 14:23).

Therefore he instructs "the strong" to renounce their Christian liberty if by making use of it they should offend the consciences of "the weak."

*

In this connection I would also make mention of the *scrupulous* or the pathologically sensitive conscience.

Here the most insignificant little thing can produce an evil conscience, in fact, a most unbearable anxiety. It may be either an insignificant act or an unguarded little word or thought.

When this once begins, it is obvious that a large number of such cases will occur every day. They come one after another in rapid succession. Such individuals are thrown directly from one spiritual conflict into another.

The result is, naturally, that they become more and more perplexed and bewildered in their conscience.

This in turn affects their whole personality. They become so distraught that they soon do not know the difference between good and evil.

They become afraid even to talk or act because they feel that nothing but wrong will come from it. At last they actually become afraid even to live.

Such supersensitive consciences we find in various stages in the development of the believer.

But we find it mostly among young and among immature Christians.

Among these it is due as a rule to a deficient understanding of the will of God. And, be it noted well, a deficient understanding not only of the various *details* of the revealed will of God, but of the very *essence* itself of the will of God. Their mind is directed as a rule to the *outward* precept and not to their inner *attitude of heart*. They do not see that it is the *motive* which is the decisive thing with God, not how the word or the act appears from the *outside*.

It becomes an embarrassing *theft* therefore in their opinion when, for instance, they go through another man's wood and cut a cane from a dry branch of an evergreen tree. A painful theft, which gives them no peace until they have confessed it to the owner. To them it becomes *falsehood* to say anything which they later in one way or another discover was not exactly true,—a lie which gives them no peace until they have confessed it to the party concerned.

We find such pathological consciences as this now and then also among older and among more mature Christians.

It is often a result of illness, or due to some mental or physical disability. In old people it is frequently due to hardening of the arteries.

A weakened nervous system naturally disposes one to such disturbances of conscience. In such cases the healing of the conscience will be conditional upon the quieting of the nerves.

In these instances therefore the cure of the *soul* must go hand in hand with the treatment of the *body*.

But there are times also when older, experienced, and more mature Christians begin to suffer from a pathological conscience, even when there is no outward physico-psychological reason for it.

In such cases we must look upon it as a form of temptation to *despair*.

During such attacks of doubt, when the believer in an exceptionally marked degree loses contact with grace that he can *feel*, his whole life in God is thrown out of balance, as it were. All spiritual values become distorted, and he tends to lose sight of them altogether. He does not seem to be able to profit any longer by his earlier Christian experiences and his previous insight into spiritual matters. Essentials and non-essentials become one confused mass as far as he is concerned.

God would teach him at such a time how impotent he is in himself in both morality and religion.

At such a time a believer encounters a special difficulty, one which arises from the fact that he is now more dependent than ever upon the consciences of others, because he cannot trust his own. Consequently he speaks with almost every one he meets about the things that are disturbing him, which only makes matters worse, because other people's views naturally differ from his.

My advice to people in this condition is that they should not consult more than *one* spiritual adviser, and preferably one who is sober-minded, experienced, and truly wise.

But consult such a person often, and be candid with him. Let him enlighten you from the Word of God and from the experience of older Christians. And ask him to impart *absolution* to you, that you may receive the help which God has given us in this outward declaration of that forgiveness of sins which it is so difficult for you in this condition to dare to believe!

If you have found a loving, wise, and firm spiritual adviser, you will with his help and intercession little by little be set free from the hindrances which are annoying you, and again come into the possession of a sound and healthy conscience.

*

In general we can say that a believer's conscience will develop, as far as its content is concerned, in the same degree as the believer permits himself to be enlightened by the Word of God concerning the will of God. The instances we have referred to are themselves sufficient to show us that the believer does not only need Christian *knowledge;* he needs above all Christian *wisdom,* that is, the ability to apply this knowledge properly to the practical relationships of life.

The development of conscience is therefore contingent fundamentally upon the believer living himself into the Word of God, particularly that part of the Word which deals with the will of God. And the more he loves the will of God, the easier it will be for him to apprehend it rightly and apply it correctly to the many complex situations which arise in life.

*

We turn now to the *practical* factor which plays such an important part in determining the development of our conscience, namely, the *will*.

In the previous chapter we have dwelt on the significance of the will in connection with the degeneration of the conscience. Here we shall note the place of the will in the growth and development of our conscience.

We begin by underscoring the fact, as observed above, that conscience according to its nature directs its mandates to the will and that it is the attitude which the will assumes towards this voice that determines the nature of the development of our conscience.

If conscience is permitted to speak unhindered, it will be *void of offense* (Acts 24:16).

This in itself means a great deal, even though this by itself does not constitute a development. All it signifies is that the conscience is not damaged, that it is intact. Here no attempt is made to silence conscience. It is permitted to warn us and judge us. We do not by our will interfere with the functioning of our conscience.

It is in this connection that the Scriptures speak of a *pure* conscience (II Timothy 1:3).

Nothing foreign to its nature is permitted to interfere with its functioning and its operations. Such people neither resist their consciences forcibly nor evade them by dishonesty.

This does not mean that consciences that are pure and void of offense can be found only in people who have no sin.

Our conscience remains void of offense and pure, even though we yield to temptation and act contrary to its warnings, provided that *after* we have been disobedient we permit our conscience to warn us, and provided that we acknowledge that it speaks the truth in whatever it says to us. And provided that we submit our wills to the behests of our conscience again, and pray God for strength to take up the battle in all earnestness once more against the particular sin to which we yielded.

A pure conscience manifests itself further when a failing and erring Christian not only acquiesces in the accusations of his conscience and accepts the reckoning when it comes, but *seeks* the reckoning.

For that reason he spends a great deal of time in prayer. He is determined that his conscience is to have the necessary quietude in which to speak to him earnestly. To prove himself is to him a daily necessity. He desires to examine especially the *motives* that have actuated his words and his actions during the day. For it has gradually become clear to him that it is easy for a spirit of guile to creep into his motives, even when he feels satisfied in his own mind that his words and his actions are outwardly in perfect order.

*

In the manner I have sketched above conscience develops and is strengthened, and that in several ways.

In the first place it becomes sensitive, that is, it is annoyed by the least little thing that conflicts with the will of God.

This *sound* sensitiveness of conscience is distinguished from the aforementioned morbid sensitiveness by the fact that it is precisely through his conscience that such a person has gained the ability to differentiate between the essential and the non-essential, and that it is through his conscience he has learned to be concerned about his motives rather than his outward acts. But the thing above all that proves that this sensitiveness is sound is the fact that conscience has entered into and become a natural part of the soul's hidden life in God. It has become a part of love's very union with God, and preserves it as a holy union.

A sensitive conscience is a precious defense for the believer. It helps him to avoid many pitfalls and many errors of which a more robust conscience would not warn him.

A sensitive conscience produces *careful* Christians, Christians who have learned, oftentimes by bitter experience, how easily our inherent sinful desires can be awakened by contact with sin in other people. That is why they walk circumspectly, and seek to avoid those situations in life which have in times past led to a fall in their lives.

For this reason they are as a rule looked upon and spoken of as being narrow-minded, pietistic, and as Christians who go to extremes. But they pay no attention to this. To them to have peace with God *in a good conscience* is more important than all else in the world.

They feel that they have suffered enough from a bad conscience, not only before their conversion, but also after. They can endure no longer the inner unrest in their relationship to God which a bad conscience produces. Regardless of cost, they are determined to be in a relationship toward God in which they are able to look at Him face to face. Only a sensitive conscience can warn them from time to time of all the things that would remove this peace and security from their lives.

Straightforwardly and erect they pursue their course in all of life's relationships. They are just as conscientious and dependable whether they are buying or selling, whether they are working for themselves or for others.

They do not say a great deal perhaps, but by their Christlike lives they influence the consciences of men more than many an eloquent speaker. They are the people who inculcate into the minds of the unconverted that respect for Christianity which is absolutely necessary before the Word of Christ can gain access to their consciences.

To me this is just the kind of Christians we are especially in need of in our day.

Comparatively, there were undoubtedly more of them generations ago. In this respect early Haugeanism stood particularly high. There was among them an imposing host of men and women in town and in country who by the conscientiousness of their lives gave incontrovertible testimony to Christianity's power to transform human life.

A robust conscience produces *careless* Christians. They need not be dishonest, not at all. On the contrary, they are often honest, warm-hearted, self-sacrificing, and energetic Christians.

But how careless they are!

Their conception of the dangers inherent in their old nature is slight indeed. Consequently they oftentimes become involved in things which affect adversely not only their own Christian life but also the cause of Christianity in general.

In their financial dealings one cannot say perhaps that they do anything that violates the law, but—there is a but!

If they have dealings with the opposite sex, one cannot say that they commit immorality of any kind, but—there is a but!

They are like clothes with a rough finish; wherever they go something always clings to them.

What these people lack above all else is a sensitive conscience to warn them of impending danger and to help them overcome the temptations which frequently cause them to stumble.

God can give us no better defense against temptation than a sensitive conscience.

The nature of temptation shows how true this is.

There is something diabolical about temptation, something satanically bewitching and bewildering. It stirs up our senses and excites our *emotions.* For the time being the forbidden thing seems more important than anything else in the world.

It weakens our *powers of judgment,* both moral and intellectual. People who are otherwise very intelligent will in a brief season of temptation commit wholly unthinkable follies,—which they often live to regret a whole lifetime afterwards.

It paralyzes our *will.* Our many good resolutions melt like wax in the hour of temptation.

All this temptation frequently does simply by being permitted to come *too close* to us.

It is like chloroform. If it gets too close to us, it will deprive us of the very possibility of offering resistance.

Here a sensitive conscience is our best defense. It utters its warnings in good season, before we have succumbed to the power of the tempter. A robust conscience, on the other hand, does not notice the danger signal before it is too late.

A sensitive conscience is also a conscience with *authority.*

The more our will submits in obedience to the voice of our conscience, the stronger and more authoritative this voice becomes, the more power it gains over our will.

As a result our daily struggle becomes greatly lessened in intensity, both when it is a question of renouncing evil as well as when it is a matter of doing good.

A conscientious Christian is thus spared many of the long and bitter struggles through which other, less conscientious, Christians must pass daily, simply because their consciences are too weak to hold in check their own wise calculations or their love of ease and pleasure.

It is like a teacher who is unable to maintain discipline. The children of whom she is in charge are egged on to all sorts of mischief and to a variety of escapades because of the absence of an authoritative voice. The result is that the teacher wastes her energy and spends a great deal of her time merely in trying to keep order.

When, on the other hand, a teacher steps into the room who possesses that mysterious gift of authority which constitutes the very essence of discipline, you can scarcely recognize these same children.

A sensitive and authoritative conscience affords the outward life of the believer clear and definite lines to follow, and spares his inner life from many a disruptive struggle and much waste of energy.

*

Thus a conscientious Christian is little by little developed.

Characteristic of him, in the first place, is that he always feels the necessity of consulting his conscience. He will not permit himself either to be enticed or frightened into acting contrary to his conscience.

In the second place, the conscientious Christian will little by little subject his whole life to his conscience as enlightened by the Word of God. The heathenish dividing up of human life into a sacred and a secular part will cease. He will permit his conscience to pass judgment on all that he does.

In this way his conscience helps him to live his whole life before God.

His daily life is thereby lifted up to a new plane; his daily life becomes his *daily spiritual service* in the most literal meaning of the word.

As it is written: "And whatsoever ye do, in word and in deed, do all in the name of the Lord Jesus, giving thanks to God the Father through him" (Colossians 3:17). "Whether therefore ye eat, or drink, or whatsoever ye do, do all to the glory of God" (I Corinthians 10:31).

Thus he will succeed in practicing real *every-day Christianity*.

Here is where the less conscientious believer fails. He looks upon his earthly calling as something worldly, and has no higher aim than to manage not to come in conflict with the civil authorities..

But that is also why his earthly calling becomes such a great temptation to him.

If he works for others, he is tempted to do his work in a lazy, careless manner and not apply himself conscientiously. If he is working for himself, he is tempted by selfish zeal and greedy desire to accumulate as much wealth as possible and bury himself in his earthly occupation.

The conscientious Christian on the other hand is happy in the thought that he has brought all his daily tasks, both great and small, into the light of his conscience and thereby also into the light of God. His desire is to do his every earthly task as before God. He has learned that everything he does in his earthly calling is a *service unto God*

*

Many people, especially young people, are never really satisfied in their earthly calling. Their work does not satisfy them. They feel inclined toward other and loftier tasks. And they strive both inwardly and outwardly to advance, to forge ahead.

A large number of such dissatisfied folk belong to the type which is never satisfied no matter where they are, and which always thinks that they are too good to be doing such menial tasks as those in which they are engaged.

There are others who have talents and interests which rightly incline them towards some other work than that in which they are engaged. Oftentimes they strive hard to get such a position and so get away from their present occupation.

In such cases this is entirely natural and justifiable. And while we are speaking about conscience in this connection, I desire to offer these dear, forward-looking young people a bit of advice.

Pray God in all confidence to lead you into the kind of work for which you feel you are best qualified. Also do what you can to get such work. God would have you make use of your talents.

But remember especially this word of Jesus: "Thou hast been faithful over a few things, I will set thee over many things" (Matthew 25:21).

Most people who desire a change of occupation forget this passage, and thus *sin* in connection with the work in which they are already engaged—first by ingratitude, next by unfaithfulness. They do their work in a careless and slipshod manner and are not conscientious in the least. Moreover, they excuse their unfaithfulness by saying that their work is not suited to them and not they to their work.

The unavoidable consequence of this is that they get in their own way and hinder their own advancement. Men do not gain confidence enough in them to have the courage to promote them. Worse, God will not promote them.

The situation is entirely different when a man does his work faithfully and conscientiously. He has the promise of God that he will be advanced. He has the promise that *God* will promote him. "I will set thee over many things," He says.

The young person who chooses to follow this course in life can look forward to a fruitful and happy life, whether his outward promotions are great or small.

In the first place, he will be happy in his work. We all derive happiness out of tasks conscientiously performed. And it is equally true that no one ever derives any happiness from a task which he performs in a careless and slipshod manner, even though he is doing a work for which he has the necessary aptitude.

In the next place, he will by his conscientious work win the gratitude, confidence, and respect of his fellow men.

And, finally, he will be to the praise of the Lord he confesses, and thus commend Him to his fellow workers. Men will, as Jesus says, "see his good works and glorify the Father who is in heaven."

Without question, men respect and appreciate the fact that we day by day do our assigned tasks in a conscientious and trustworthy manner more than any other good deed we might perform.

We have many Christian young people in our country today.

We also have many young people with a will to work, who have a purpose in their work, and who really are workers.

If these young folk could all see the importance of conscientious, every-day Christianity and put it first upon the working program of their lives, it would not be long before it would leave ineffaceable traces in the Christian life and work of America.

In fact, Christian work in our country would see a *new day*.

*

Finally I would mention the importance of a sensitive and an authoritative conscience in connection with our life in God itself. It is nothing less than the condition upon which our hidden life in God can become fruitful and happy.

In the first place, a sensitive conscience will impel us to seek the cross of Christ. We will see and feel sin as such a living reality that the cross will be our most precious refuge every day.

And that is all that is necessary for us in order to live fruitfully in the grace of God.

God's boundless grace surrounds us on every hand, and would enter into our lives. "Behold, I stand at the door and knock; if any man hear my voice and open the door, I will come in to him, and will sup with him and he with me" (Revelation 3:20).

In the second place, a sensitive conscience will impel us to seek *intimate fellowship* with the Lord. A sensitive conscience, as we know, reproves us for even the least little wrong that we do, and gives us no peace until we have confessed it to God.

In this way our daily life becomes an unbroken conversation with God in all quietness. Our soul is helped by a sensitive conscience into a most confidential and intimate relationship with God.

In the third place, a sensitive conscience will, through these full and regular reconciliations with God, make place in our hearts for the *peace of God* which passes all understanding (Philippians 4:7).

Even the prophet of old knew this: "Oh that thou hadst hearkened to my commandment! Then had thy peace been as a river, and thy righteousness as the waves of the sea" (Isaiah 48:18).

This is the blessed condition to which we refer when we speak of *peace with God* in a *good* conscience.

One can have peace with God also without a good conscience.

For when the Scriptures speak of peace with God they mean something deeper and something more than we ordinarily mean by the expression. We usually think in this connection of *our* relationship *to God,* more particularly of the quiet, peaceful, and happy state of soul which we enjoy in fellowship with the Lord.

The Scriptures, meanwhile, speak first and foremost of *God's* relationship *to us,* of the fact that God, who before was in a relationship to us in which His wrath was upon us, has now made peace with us. Thus Romans 5:1. And in *this* relationship of peace we have a part as long as we are children of God, regardless of our spiritual state, whether it be quiet and peaceable or not.

A Christian therefore has peace with God in the sense here referred to also during his seasons of spiritual weakness and disobedience, as long as guile has not been permitted to enter into his spirit,—but *without* a good conscience!

A dull conscience leads only to half-way reconciliations with God. As a result the soul will not find *rest* in the grace of God. God's Spirit will make such a soul *restless.* He would thereby seek to rouse him from his spiritual stupor. During this time the Spirit cannot therefore bear witness with his spirit that he is a child of God. Nor can He bring forth in the sinner's heart the childlike Abba-Father cry (Romans 8:15-16).

He, on the other hand, who is impelled by a sensitive conscience to make a full accounting before God every day, will experience peace with God in a *good* conscience, that which the Scriptures call "the *mystery* of faith in a *good conscience*" (I Timothy 3:9).

And he will live as a consequence thereof in a secure and unstrained relationship both toward God and man.

The inner life of such Christians takes on an ease and a candor which gradually manifests itself also in their outward being, in the expression of their eyes, in their ways, and in all their associations with their fellow men. They take on unconsciously a free-born and noble bearing, which endows them with characteristic attractiveness.

This also assures us in its own silent language that it is conscience which makes man a man.